SETTING UP HOME

SALLY KING
and
JOYCE LOWRIE

FREDERICK MULLER LIMITED
LONDON

To Jonathan and Stephen

First published in Great Britain in 1982 by Frederick Muller Limited, Dataday House, Alexandra Road, Wimbledon, London, SW19 7JU.

Copyright © Sally King and Joyce Lowrie 1982

All rights reserved. No part of this publication may be reproduced, stored in a retrieval system, or transmitted, in any form or by any means, electronic, mechanical, photocopying, recording or otherwise, without the prior consent of Frederick Muller Limited.

British Library Cataloguing in Publication Data

King, Sally + Lowrie, Joyce
   Setting up home.
   1. Dwellings—Remodelling 2. Home economics
   I. Title   II. Lowrie, Joyce
   643'.7   TH4816

ISBN 0-584-11015-4

Typeset by Texet, Leighton Buzzard, Bedfordshire.
Printed in Great Britain by The Anchor Press Ltd., Colchester, Essex

Contents

1 Your launching pad   6
— Do some research before coming to decisions and be prepared to be flexible
— Develop a business-like approach
   Seven things which repay investment
   Five things which do not usually repay investment
— Think like a nomad

2 The financial angle   13
— How big a mortgage?
— What type of mortgage?
— Where to get your mortgage?
— Where to save?
— The unavoidable extras

3 House-hunting   27
— Decide on your price range
— Decide on the area
— Decide on what type of house or flat
— Starting the hunt
— Check-list for the house-hunter
— Steps to take to buy a place
— Buying a house at auction
— Buying by tender
— The procedure for buying in Scotland

4 Getting the basics right   39
— The fabric
— Services
— Insulation
— The heating

5 Exploiting the style you've got   52
— Four typical English house styles
   The suburban semi
   The post-war modern
   Late Victorian/the Edwardian
   Tiny cottage/small terrace house
— Making your own imprint
— Putting together colour
— Style for as little as possible
   Floor
   Walls
   Windows
   Doors
   Lighting

6 Exploiting the space you've got   67
— How to make your own plan
— Exploiting the space without making structural changes
— Structural changes that will cost hundreds not thousands

7 One-room living   73
Minimum sizes
   — Some alternative plans
   — Making your own plans
   — To divide up the space or not?
The basic essentials
   — The dual-purpose approach
   — The essentials of storage
   — Things which fit in small spaces
   — Conclusions

8 Living rooms to live in   89
- Making it as spacious as possible
- Alternative heating
- Comfortable seating
- Focal points
- Shelving and tables
- Pianos
- Eating in the living room
- Lighting for living
- Floors

9 Starter kitchens   97
- Some basic kitchen plans
- Assessing the basic necessities, cooker, etc.
- Making the kitchen work
- What you need to store and how to store it

10 The basic bedroom   105
- Choosing the bed
- Bedclothes to suit the bed
- Storage in the bedroom
- Making the bedroom work

11 Beautifying the bathroom   111
- Some cosmetic changes
- Renovating existing appliances
- Planning a new bathroom
- Fitting in some extras
- When to contact the Local Authority

12 In-and-out-doors   118
- Creating an 'outdoors' indoors
- Halfway outdoors — the window box, balcony, hanging basket, etc.
- The room outside
- The bigger garden
- Basic care for the outside fabric

13 What you can do if you try   125
- Painting the walls and ceilings
- Wallpapering the walls
- Decorating the woodwork
- Floor treatments — sanding then sealing or painting
- Floor treatments — laying hardboard
- Floor treatments — laying sheet vinyl and foam backed carpet
- Making your own curtains
- Five ways to improve insulation
- Fixing shelving, units, curtain rails to walls
- Ceramic tiles

14 Planning your housekeeping   136
The major shopping
- Don't rush into things — do your research
- Picking things up cheap
- Getting some credit
- Your rights as a consumer

Day-to-day shopping v the weekly expedition
- Cash-and-carry stores
- Supermarkets
- Freezer centres
- P-Y-O fruit and veg
- Markets
- Use your initiative

A new approach to food
- Keeping yourself healthy
- Putting all this into practice
- Simplicity is now the key to entertaining

Useful Addresses   **157**

Further Reading   **158**

Index   **159**

SETTING UP HOME

1 Your launching pad

Setting up house for the first time is one of life's milestones.

For the first time you have to grapple with estate agents, the district surveyor, solicitors, plumbers, not-too-keen mortgagors and definitely recalcitrant builders. It can feel like you're David v the Goliaths.

You face problems like easements, rising damp, structural cracks, small-bore pipes, ring mains and alternative fuels. Fortunate are they who did a CSE in carpentry.

You have to make decisions about floors — should you choose carpets, vinyl, cork, Amtico, stripped boards or just leave it? Walls — to be papered in Laura Ashley sprigs, or dragged Jocasta Innes-style? Colours? Not to mention what curtains, beds, sofas, tables, glasses, saucepans and a hundred and one other things you are going to have to live with and like (or replace) for maybe the next twenty years.

Suddenly you have to be as expert as the experts on a whole spectrum of skills and expertise you have probably had no cause to think about until now.

We are going to try and show you the ropes about all this sort of thing from the inside. But we're also going to try and go further because really this expertise is only the means to an end: owning and living in your own place.

We see setting up house as a milestone in other senses too. Certainly the first time is different from subsequent times.

You've come to the important moment in your life when, having cut loose from home, got a job and so on, you are ready to live independently in a home of your own creation. You are probably just married — or about to be. Or maybe you're

embarking on your own. Or with friends. Or with what the US census delicately describes as a POSSLQ*. Or, come to that, a PSSSLQ. In setting up house you're launching out to create your own chosen style of living in accordance with your aims in life.
Two difficulties arise at this stage for almost everyone:

1. What is your style of living? You may not be sure since for most of us it evolves slowly as we live. Its relation to your home is like the setting to a drama in the theatre. The drama is provided by your life, work and relationships; the setting (helping or hindering) is your home. Just as set designers have to have some appreciation of what the drama is about, you have to know enough about yourself to formulate your aims and needs to provide them with a satisfactory setting. Some people have an absolutely clear idea of their style. They know that they are really Jane Austens/self-sufficient cottagers/mediaeval monks/liberated Victorians/comfortable muddlers/pop musicians — and take off from there. Most of us are not so positive and have to find out as we go along.

2. You are not exactly awash with funds. Even if you know exactly what you want, you are unlikely to be buying your ideal house — whether that's a Georgian gem, Tudor mansion or penthouse flat. You're buying what you can afford and you want to make the most of it. Sooner or later you'll want to sell it and, when you do, you'll want your next home to be a step up — bigger, more privacy, better proportions, nicer area, 100ft garden or whatever. Meantime you have to get value for money, select carefully, decide on priorities.

But you are absolutely right to make the effort to buy your own place because this is putting your foot on the first rung of the property-owning ladder. If you handle it right your home can become a better investment of your time and money than most shares, many jobs and even bona fide businesses.

Coming to terms with these two problems before you buy, let alone fix up, any place helps you make the most of what you've got. Nothing, no-one can give you foolproof answers. You have to make your own mistakes. We all do. The second time round you know what works for you; you have found out some things to avoid. The first time around you can only try and think ahead, as clearly as you are able. Here are some guidelines:

*Persons of Opposite Sex Sharing Living Quarters. Person of Same Sex ditto

Do some research before coming to decisions and be prepared to be flexible

An architect taking on any commission to design a house or conversion tries to get an insight into all aspects of the client's life. We are going to try and show you, in each relevant section, the sort of questions you might ask yourself. For instance, what to ask yourself before you even start looking for your place is at the beginning of the chapter on house-hunting.

One thing which will affect your choice almost as much as what you can afford is how much you can do yourself. The more you can do, the more money you save. Obviously, because you only pay for materials and not the expensive labour. We think there is a lot anyone can do if they try. We discuss how to set about it in the last chapter. But anyone who has (even reluctantly) taken the woodworking or dressmaking option at school can attempt more. The point is many things don't require much skill. The difference between your performance and the builder's is often just a matter of time taken. He is a lot quicker at it, but his results are not necessarily better. If you are at all practical and can follow instructions as given in manuals like the ones produced by *Reader's Digest* Do-It-Yourself series you can tackle a surprisingly wide range of jobs.

Develop a business-like approach

Try to think in terms of return on your investment. (But not to the extent of ending up with a spec-builder's dream — tailored to everyone's taste but your own!)

For the past twenty years houses and flats have been an extremely good investment. While retail prices have risen to four times what they were in 1960, house prices are, even now, on average, twelve times what they were. And all the capital gains you make on your main house/home are tax free.

Here are some things which we think repay investment and some we don't, to show you what we mean:

Seven things which repay investment
1. Structural and basic improvements — such as damp courses, re-wiring, good roofs, elimination of woodworm, dry rot, etc. These pay for themselves in the sense that when you sell, buyers will tend to knock the cost of putting right such basic defects as these off the price.
2. Improvements which reduce running costs. At the recent Homeworld exhibition at Milton Keynes, nearly every exhibition house claimed to be energy-saving whether it really was or not.

Cheap ways of saving, like extra insulation (see chapter 4, page 44) in the roof, round doors and window frames, hot tank, exposed pipes and D-I-Y double glazing will certainly repay you. More expensive forms like elaborate double-glazing, less likely to do so. Heating which is flexible (see chapter 4, page 49) with choice of fuels and an open fire somewhere is better than using a single fuel because fuel prices change so arbitrarily and are affected by strikes, shortages, etc. But to put in an alternative specially, like solar panels, would not repay you for at least five years.

3. People often choose one house or flat rather than another because they fall in love with one big room. Your house or flat is a better proposition both for you to live in and to sell later on if you concentrate on making one room really good. Don't spend too much. The effect of plants, light, space and order is often enough.

4. The front of the house and entrance affects people disproportionately too. Keeping it well painted is worth while. Minor improvements to make the entrance pleasant, well-lit and welcoming are worth while — lights, doorbell in order, suitable knobs, knockers, letter boxes, etc. Major works are not usually sensible.

5. Do modernise the kitchen and bathroom — but in moderation. People certainly buy more willingly if they can walk into a kitchen and cook, or take a bath, the day they move in. But the Poggenpohl kitchen and the Bonsack bathroom with expensive floor to ceiling tiling will hardly get your money back in luxury houses and flats, let alone your first place.

6. However small the garden or patio, tame it so it is a pleasant leafy place to sit. This costs very little (see page 122). (You always can remove your pretty garden furniture when you go.)

7. Some of the small structural ways to make the most of your space we suggest in chapter 5 (page 67).

Five things which do not usually repay investment

1. Going one better than the Joneses. Every neighbourhood, estate or even street of similar houses or flats in a block has its own price range. If you spend so much on doing it up and lift your house out of its price range, you'll find it hard recouping. You can't count on neighbourhoods 'coming up' either. In the end areas are often transformed, but for every one that is, there is another that has been blighted by motorway or council plans. The Kings' first two-up-two-down in Battersea illustrates the uncertainties of waiting for somewhere to 'come-up'. Twenty years ago a planning blight descended on the area when the council decreed it was 'scheduled for redevelopment'. We sold our modernised house to the council at the standard price for those houses in those days. The area has not after all been redeveloped, but for half that time our house was bricked up and unoccupied. It is only in the last year or two that the council changed its plans and the houses have been selling briskly at twenty times the price we got. Our house has been finally re-occupied. This is the sort of time-scale and uncertainty you have to be prepared for.

2. Building-on. This pays only in the long run and if, by so doing, you substantially improve the accommodation. It should be of as lasting a quality as the house and preferably hoist you into a different price bracket — i.e. from a three to four-bed house in estate agent terms. Ditto building-up.

3. Building-in — elaborate cupboards, shelves, units (except in the kitchen and bathroom, and keep these to a minimum). Estate agents make a big play on "Wealth of 'robes'" in their ads, but you probably won't get your money back in under ten years. You would be better off spending the same money on moveable cupboard units or nice free-standing furniture, which you can take with you when you go. We have some friends who built-in *all* their cupboards in their first house, which they had converted themselves. When they moved, five years and two children later, to their second, bigger house they had to build their storage in all over again because they could not take their storage with them.

4. Building a garage. Creating a parking space in an otherwise unused space if the house/flat is in a restricted parking area is valuable. Otherwise the cost of building a garage won't repay you in the short term, even if you got a pre-fab.

5. Extravaganzas (like saunas and jacuzzis) or specialist goodies (like conservatories, dark rooms or Aga cookers). These will be fun for you, but there's only a chance in a million that someone wanting them will be around when you're ready to sell.

It may seem a little cold-blooded to think of selling when you are only setting up — and for the first time too. But these are factors you have to keep in mind when you're choosing between alternatives, just as you also keep in mind your individual needs and personal tastes. Thinking like this makes decisions easier in the end.

Think like a nomad

Taking the value for money approach one step further, we suggest you could do worse than to think of your home and possessions rather in the way nomads do theirs. Think of the beautiful carpets, rugs and furnishings the Tuareg nomads make for themselves. A lot of work as well as wealth is invested in these possessions. Every time they move on and pitch tent in a new place, they set up their own home, full of beautiful and cared-for objects. If you've spent a lot of time choosing something or making it, or even just growing to love it, it makes sense to be able to enjoy it wherever you're living.

Today it is much less likely that you will stay in one house/flat all your life than it used to be. Mortgages, on average, last only seven years. Your job, or just your career blossoming and your horizons widening, will make it unlikely that your house-owning pattern will follow that of landed gentry — one home for generations. So it makes sense to direct as much of the love and effort you spend on your first home as practicable, on things which you will be able to take away with you when you move. The very best of these will form a sort of core of your household possessions. Some might even have formed the core of your parents' or grandparents' homes. Your core will eventually range from pieces of furniture you especially like, through pictures and objects right down to kitchen things you find indispensable. As you start gathering the necessities of living around you, consider them in this way before finally choosing. For instance, just as we have pointed out that moveable furniture makes more sense than building-in, the same applies to choosing rugs instead of fitted carpets, a moveable cooker rather than a built-in hob and oven.

A guide to what you can and can't take with you is the definition of the fixtures you are obliged to leave behind you when you move. Anything that is part of the fabric of the house is sold with it. This includes, of course, built-in cupboards and units; plumbing and heating installations which are part of the structure of the house; gas or electric instantaneous water heaters; garden sheds and greenhouses built on foundations; and electric wall sockets, switches and wiring and sockets as far as the appliance; plants and trees in the garden. Grey areas, where you are wise to discuss what is being sold or not with the buyer/estate agent/solicitor, are curtain rails and tracks, fitted shelves not indissolubly fixed to the walls, front door fittings such as knobs, knockers and chimes, and the TV aerial on the roof. The rest you take.

Setting up house is not all calculation. We are just aiming to show you how to calculate and so avoid some mistakes. But as we have said, nobody gets it right all the time. You have to be prepared to admit to mistakes — or even the need for a change. Starting a family will mean you have to alter all sorts of things, but you can't envisage every contingency and plan ahead for it in detail. You can only make plans which are flexible and possible to adapt without too much disruption.

Part of the fun of setting up house is that you get a whole new range of interests. So many doors are opened, you find you have talents you may never have suspected. As your life develops so can your home.

In this book we will take you through the stages of finding and setting up a first place of your own with these guiding principles in mind. We start with the essential requirements — getting the money together and finding the house or flat. We discuss the basics you have to get right (which you can skip if the house is new and/or the surveyor has given you an A1 report). Then we discuss how to make the most of the space generally and of each room in particular. We also show how to simplify the chores and routines of everyday living. Finally we show you how to set about doing things for yourself, even if you have never picked up a paintbrush since you were at primary school.

The financial angle 2

Buying a house is not only the biggest, but also the best investment most of us ever make. That doesn't alter the fact that getting the money together for the first time has ever been anything but a struggle. This book can't do much to ease your struggle, but by going through some of the alternatives, it might help you avoid making expensive mistakes.

Nearly everyone buys their home on a mortgage of some kind (that's the loan you get to buy it and what you have to pay back eventually). You have to persuade some institution (like a bank or a building society) to lend you the cash. You also have to have saved quite a substantial amount of additional cash. This is partly because you may not get a mortgage large enough to cover the complete cost of the property; partly because there are all the unavoidable expenses you incur in the process of buying property; and partly because you are going to need some money to set yourselves up, however frugally.

The questions you might ask yourself are:

1. How big a mortgage can I expect?
2. What type of mortgage is most suitable?
3. Who, when the time comes, should be approached for money?
4. Where is the best place to save?

The problem is that the mortgage situation can vary so much in a comparatively short time. For instance, as we write, mortgages are readily available, but not so long ago there was a 'famine' and building societies would only consider lending to people who had saved with them for at least six months. Until the banks entered the home loan field, 100% mortgages were very

SETTING UP HOME

uncommon, now they are less so. Government policies affect the amount of money available and the interest rates, but you cannot always foretell how.

So it pays to be aware of what the situation is when you start saving, but to be prepared to be opportunistic when the moment to arrange the mortgage arrives.

How big a mortgage?

You are limited in what you can borrow by what the people you borrow from judge you are able to repay.

The usual rule of thumb is the income test. You can borrow two and a half times your annual income (e.g. if you earn £5,000 p.a. you can borrow £12,500). Some institutions don't lend so much, others rise to more — but seldom as much as three times your income.

For couples with two incomes, most lenders will take the second income into account, but not at the same rate. The typical adjustment is two and a half times the higher income plus once the lower income (e.g. if income A is £10,000 and income B £5,000, the total loan would be £30,000). *Money Which?* (December 1980) listed the lending policies of the nineteen biggest building societies and found twelve different adjustments.

Another test is the outgoings test. This makes the assumption that what you earn in a week is the maximum you ought to repay in a month (e.g. if you get £100 a week and aim to repay £100 a month, this represents a mortgage of around £11,000). The same allowances are made for two incomes in the same way (e.g. two and a half times the higher plus the lower).

These are rough guides only. The effects of inflation, which will devalue in real terms what you are repaying, as well as the possibility that your income may go up substantially as your career develops, sometimes make it seem sensible to take on as big a mortgage as possible. But remember, mortgage repayments are relentless and to some extent at the mercy of interest rates (e.g. on a £10,000 loan over twenty-five years when the interest rate is 12% the monthly repayments are around £106; when it goes up to 14% they go up to £120.) You have to go on repaying, whatever your personal circumstances.

When the time comes to apply for a mortgage, the exact figures will be worked out by whoever is making you the loan.

THE FINANCIAL ANGLE

What type of mortgage?

There are two main ways of repaying a mortgage. The one you choose will partly depend on what your income tax level is — and what it is likely to be in the not-so-distant future. Your tax comes into it because what you pay in interest on the first £25,000 borrowed on your own home (but not your second home, holiday cottage or condominium in Florida) qualifies for tax relief. Up until April 1983 PAYE coding is adjusted to take this into account. After that the situation changes, though, as we write, details are not finalised. You will pay your interest net of tax so if you pay income tax at the standard rate, your PAYE coding will not be affected. It will be arranged between the mortgagee and the Inland Revenue. However arrangements for loans of over £25,000 and for people paying tax at the higher rates will probably remain on the present basis.

What the £10,000 mortgage costs

Some approximate comparisons. Assuming the applicant is thirty, healthy, etc. and the mortgage is due to run twenty-five years. Costs are roughly pro rata but the large mortgages usually start at higher rates of interest.

Type of mortgage		Total net cost per month Person paying tax at 30%	Person paying tax at 60%	Estimated cash at end (see note)
Repayment mortgage				
1. Interest rate 15%	1st yr	£ 91.40	£ 53.90	—
	10th yr	94.36	59.52	
	20th yr	106.95	84.99	
2. Interest rate 12½%	1st yr	78.75	47.50	
	10th yr	82.02	54.05	
	20th yr	93.28	76.56	
3. Interest rate 10%	1st yr	66.90	41.90	
	10th yr	70.33	48.76	
	20th yr	79.90	67.90	
With-profits Endowment mortgage				
1. Interest rate 15½%		122.93	84.18	£ 22820
2. Interest rate 13%		108.34	75.84	22820
3. Interest rate 10%		93.76	67.51	22820
Low-cost With-profits Endowment mortgage				
1. Interest rate 15½%		103.89	65.14	2830
2. Interest rate 13%		89.30	56.50	2830
3. Interest rate 10½%		74.72	48.47	2830
Non-profit Endowment mortgage				
1. Interest rate 15½%		108.14	69.39	—
2. Interest rate 13%		93.55	61.05	—
3. Interest rate 10½%		78.97	52.72	—
Option mortgages (tax relief on interest not applicable)		Cost per Month		
Repayment mortgage at 10½% (instead of 15%)		£ 95.40	—	
at 8¾% (instead of 12½%)		83.20	—	
at 7% (instead of 10%)		71.60	—	
Low-cost With-profits Endowment mortgage				
at 11% (instead of 15½%)		105.14		2830
at 9¼% (instead of 13%)		90.55		2830
at 7¼% (instead of 10½%)		73.89		2830

We have to thank Douglas Hayden of Douglas Hayden and Company, Insurance Brokers, for supplying us with these figures.

SETTING UP HOME

The repayment mortgage
You borrow the whole sum and every month you pay interest on the loan itself and repay some of the loan. As, by some unbelievably complicated arithmetic, your repayments are calculated so they are the same throughout the life of the mortgage (as long as the interest rate doesn't change), you are paying large sums of interest and making very small repayments on the original loan in the first years. One advantage of this is that during those first years you benefit more from tax relief, so the actual cost of your mortgage is less early on. Another advantage is that many building societies will adjust the mortgage if the interest rate goes up too steeply by lengthening the time over which you repay. (The calculations are shown in great detail in the Consumer Association's book, *Raising the Money to Buy your House*.)

One disadvantage is that if you end or change the mortgage in its early years, you find you have paid back very little of the original loan (e.g. in the first year you are unlikely to have paid back £50 of a £10,000 mortgage).

The option repayment mortgage
If you don't pay tax, you obviously can't benefit from any tax concessions. The option mortgage scheme was started in 1968 to help people like you. You get a repayment mortgage in the same way but pay a lower rate of interest and the government makes up the difference in a subsidy to whoever made you the loan.

Your monthly repayments will, obviously, be affected by changes in the interest rate but tax concessions will not affect them. You also pay off the capital slightly faster which is a small bonus when you move.

You can opt into or out of the scheme; your mortgage adviser can give you all the details.

The endowment mortgage
With endowment mortgages, the loan to buy your house is linked to an endowment assurance plan.

Each month you pay only interest on the basic loan, plus a premium to an insurance company. This is your 'endowment' and when it matures (as it is timed to when the term of the mortgage ends) you use it to pay off the capital all in one go. The advantage to high-rate tax payers is that all the monthly repayments are either interest (with full tax concessions) or insurance premiums (which are paid after deduction of tax at a reduced rate — at present 15%).

There are three main types of endowment mortgage:

a. The Without-profits scheme, which aims to provide exactly the sum of money you need to pay off your mortgage when the time comes.

b. The With-profits scheme, which gives you a more expensive 'endowment', but you benefit from the bonuses declared by the insurance company while your policy runs and you reckon to end up with a substantial lump sum more than you need to pay off the mortgage.

c. The Low-cost With-profits endowment is a relatively new invention. It costs you a good deal less than a with-profits policy, and often less than a without-profits policy, but (by counting in the bonuses) gives you enough to pay off your loan plus some additional cash. This is the most often recommended type of endowment mortgage today.

Any endowment mortgage has a higher rate of interest than a normal building society repayment mortgage does. There may also be a premium rate for higher loans, difficult houses, etc. There is no set formula. Each mortgage gets individual quotes.

An advantage is that if you want to move, your mortgage arrangements can usually be transferred to the next house, with a second, top-up policy added on if necessary.

The disadvantages are that the term cannot be extended to mitigate the effects of higher repayments when interest rates go up. Also, if you decide to end the policy prematurely, you are apt to get a disagreeable surprise because you often won't get back what you have put in, never mind any bonuses.

The option mortgage linked to an endowment policy
If you do not pay tax, you can apply the option mortgage principle to the interest payments you make on an endowment policy. You will have to repay the tax you have deducted from the premiums.

Where to get your mortgage?

Whatever type of mortgage you decide on, you've got to find the purchase price of the house or flat you want to buy.

Many people do their own leg-work and find their own mortgages — the more determined with the aid of one or other of the very comprehensive books produced by the publishers of *Which?* in their hands. Others with no time, throw their problem at an insurance broker or mortgage broker and see what he comes up with.

The building societies
75% of mortgages are granted through the building societies. There are over 200 with over 8,000 branches. You can get a list of members and an excellent free booklet *Building Societies and House Purchase* from the Building Societies Association. Or you can stick to the ones in your local high street.

Most building society mortgages are the repayment type, but societies can arrange an endowment mortgage. They also arrange the option mortgage.

Although (like Tolstoy's happy families) all building societies seem alike, in practice they differ. They are a very British institution. They started in the late eighteenth century when groups of working men pooled their resources to build themselves homes. When they were all housed their society was terminated. Some societies lived on because the groups saw they would get their housing quicker if they took in savings (and paid interest on them) from outsiders who did not want to be housed but had got savings.

Since 1836, activities of building societies have been regulated by Act of Parliament. But their aim in life (to take in savings and from these to finance house purchases for other people) remains, broadly speaking, the same.

This background may explain why every building society has slightly different rules and the branch managers have so much individual discretion. Because this is so, it is a good idea to talk to the branch manager of a society before you start placing your savings at his branch.

The ease of getting money from a building society is largely influenced by the economic climate — which affects how much money they have to lend. But other factors which might affect your mortgage, particularly in difficult times, could be:

a. The priority given to savers and in particular any special help given to first-time buyers. Some societies have special schemes.

b. The type of house you want. Some societies have been less than enthusiastic about houses built pre-1919, flats in conversions, and property which needs a lot doing to it, but most are now much more open-minded than they used to be.

c. The locality. While some societies will lend on inner city property, others are not so keen. Some small societies only lend on places in their own area — which is not much use if your job takes you elsewhere.

d. Their attitude to you and your income will also colour what they will lend you.

These are important questions to ask because although you have to pay the full price of the property, all these considerations influence the building society's decision as to how much — or what percentage of the selling price — they will advance. Usually it's 80% but it can go higher — even to 100% for some societies' deals for first-timers. If the advance is over 80% societies require some additional security — usually this takes the form of an Indemnity by an Insurance company for which a single premium is payable.

Another limitation is that societies cannot by law allocate more than 10% of their funds to loans exceeding £37,500. Many charge a higher rate of interest on loans over £25,000.

In hard times there is a strong link between saving with a building society and being granted a mortgage. So it does pay to shop around for the society which seems to suit your needs best.

The high street banks

Banks have only recently stopped being rather stand-offish about mortgages. Now, awash with funds, they are competing for your custom. (Barclays' 1982 Getting Married Scheme guarantees a mortgage to people who have saved at least £1,000 within at least a year, of ten times what they have saved — subject to the house being suitable and the 2½ times earnings rule.) Most banks also emphasize that you need not even have been a customer, let alone saved with them, to apply for a mortgage.

As with building societies, the local branch manager has quite a lot of discretion. Their criteria of credit-worthiness is the same two and a half times income plus some allowance for the second income. Banks also do their own valuations and normally give 80% purchase price but up to 90% for first-time buyers. But they lend larger sums than building societies like to consider. Some have a mortgage minimum of £10,000. So if you want a large mortgage you may do best to approach a bank.

You can opt for an endowment or a repayment mortgage — or an option mortgage — through a bank.

Other financial institutions

There are also insurance companies, finance houses, other banks (foreign or secondary) who sometimes give mortgages, or bridge the gap between the mortgage you get and the amount you actually need to purchase your property or put it into good repair. Finding these sources and working out the deal is where the mortgage broker (see below) comes into his own. (Not even the Consumer's Association attempts to unravel this maze!)

Local authorities

One tends to forget that not so long ago, when the local authorities were spending freely, they were a good bet for mortgages on property in their areas, indeed often on property the building societies would not consider. Today, most have to restrict their credit to council tenants with a legal right to buy their house/flat on a local authority mortgage. If you are in this fortunate position don't look further afield.

When life gets brighter for local authorities, they might be worth approaching because:

a. They are often glad to lend on houses in run-down areas — especially if you propose to turn one house into two or more units.

b. They often gave a higher proportion of the value — like 100% when everyone was offering 80% maximum.

c. They accepted a long term of repayment — thirty years rather than the normal twenty-five.

The interest a council can charge is government-controlled as is the maximum they can lend (£25,000 at present). However, through the Building Societies' Support Scheme, the councils can nominate candidates to a society. To benefit you must be nominated by your council. You must also have sufficient income to make the repayments (the two and a half times rule again).

New town development corporations

If your work moves you to a New Town (like Milton Keynes) or even if you just want to live there, you are positively encouraged to buy a house if not actually helped.

One scheme which helps people setting up for the first time

who can't manage the full price of a mortgage, is shared ownership. The corporation sells half the house and rents you the other half. You pay them a small rent for this half until you can afford to take on the whole house. Enquiries to the appropriate development corporation offices.

Other sources
Some employers — banks, building societies, insurance companies, for example — give special facilities for mortgages to their employees. (You often pay a lower rate of interest for instance.) If this is true of your employer, you have struck lucky.

One caveat: find out what, if anything, happens to your mortgage if you change your job, or move house.

Equally lucky are those whose families help them. Occasionally solicitors know of private trusts willing to invest in your mortgage.

Wherever you get your money, it is important to make sure the terms are as reasonable as they would be were you fixing up your mortgage with a bank or building society. Sometimes, for example, private loans are called in (you have to pay up) suddenly. You want to make sure you are given enough notice, if this happens, to re-arrange your affairs. You should get a solicitor to check the agreement for you, even if you are borrowing from close relatives.

Whoever you borrow from, the kind of mortgage you opt for, and the interest you are charged, the tax concessions on the interest remains the same.

Finding your mortgage through a mortgage broker
A mortgage broker, or an insurance broker who also deals in mortgages, is a fixer — invaluable because they can often find money for you when you can't, when you haven't time to do the leg-work or when you haven't started to save.

Although both insurance and mortgage brokers can fix up any type of mortgage, there is a difference between what they charge for their services. Mortgage brokers invariably charge a fee of 2%. Insurance brokers normally only charge a fee on repayment mortgages; on endowment mortgages they are remunerated by the commission they receive from the insurance company on the endowment policy.

By law, from December 31st 1981, all insurance brokers

SETTING UP HOME

have to be registered with the Insurance Brokers Registration Council before they can trade. Their code of conduct is designed among other things to protect you from rogues who demand money on account, fix up illegal deals, abscond, etc. You can also check a broker's membership of either the British Insurance Broker's Association or the Corporation of Mortgage, Finance and Life Assurance Brokers. This would also be an indication of a broker's professional standing.

Where to save?

"Most young people should start planning to buy a home of their own as soon as they leave school."

THE PENGUIN BOOK OF MONEY by *Fingleton and Ticknell*, 1980.

Perhaps that is expecting too much! But we have seen how saving is sometimes linked in the building society world with getting a mortgage. Banks are beginning to offer similar inducements. The government has even inaugurated a Homeloan Scheme for first-time buyers who have saved for two years.

Certainly if you plan your savings strategically you will have a better chance of getting a mortgage when you need one whatever the economic climate. You will not be so restricted on the price of the house or so dependent on a good valuation by whoever is lending the money. You will not have to sacrifice furnishings in order to pay for all the unavoidable extras buying a house always incurs.

The Homeloan Scheme

Started by the government in 1978 to help people buy their first home. If you save for two years, you get some cash benefits and the option of an additional loan which is interest-free for five years.

It is for lower-priced property. The ceiling prices are fixed by the government and change from time to time.

It works very simply. When you start saving you tell the bank or whoever that you will wish to take advantage of the Homeloan Scheme and you get a form to fill in. This makes you eligible for the benefits.

Institutions taking part in the scheme are building societies, banks, Trustee Savings Bank, friendly societies, the National Girobank, the National Savings Bank and Ulster Savings. These all have details of the scheme.

The benefits depend on the amount you save. The bonus (April 1981) amounts to £40 if you have kept £300 at least in your savings account during the twelve months before you apply for your benefit and £110 if you have had £1,000 or more. You also qualify for an interest-free loan of £600 which you do not start repaying for five years.

Two of you can save in separate accounts, but you only get one bonus and loan on the one property you are buying jointly.

If this seems too little inducement or you want to buy a more expensive property than the Homeloan Scheme will allow, you should follow up the deals offered by some of the banks and the building societies.

Advantages of saving with a building society
The building societies feel that 'when the demand for mortgage funds exceeds the supply it is not unreasonable for societies to give preference to their own investors and this they do'.(BSA booklet)

From the point of view of interest and security, building societies are good places to save. They are completely safe — you can't lose your savings in some dreadful collapse if they are members of the BSA. It is also advantageous if you pay tax at the basic rate. There is a deal with the Inland Revenue so that interest on a building society account comes to you already taxed, but the rate at which it is taxed is a notional one and a little lower than the basic rate. So when they say 8.5%, that's what you get. (If you pay tax at higher rates you do have to pay higher rates on your building society interest. If you don't pay tax at all you can't get back the tax paid by the Society.)

Most people use the ordinary share accounts, or their equivalent, which are simple to put money into and take it out. There are other savings schemes run by societies with higher rates of interest, but some have to run for a number of years to give their full benefit while others need one month's notice of withdrawal. Schemes worth looking out for are those which set out to give positive help to first-time buyers. But make sure that the society who gets your money is the one most likely to give you the mortgage you want. Shop around. Check up. Move your money into another society if suddenly it offers better terms. Be an opportunist.

SETTING UP HOME

Other places to save

Banks are beginning to offer to finance mortgages with schemes linked to savings.

Bank deposit accounts have the advantage of being very flexible — you can get at your money easily. They may seem to offer higher rates than the building societies, but remember, you pay tax on any interest.

£1,400 put into a National Savings Bank Account (the old Post Office Savings under a new name) will get you £70 interest free of tax — a minor boon only to those in the higher brackets.

There are many savings schemes on offer which promise much higher rates of interest. Many of these you'll find commit you to keeping your money in for a specific term and often unless it's in for the full term you don't get the full benefit. When you are saving up for your first home, you are well-advised to keep your options open. Two years is too long to keep your money tied up. You need to be able to use it when the opportunity presents itself.

The unavoidable extras

Just buying a house or flat and organising a mortgage involves a lot of expense — estimated at 2% of the purchase price.

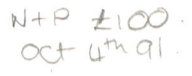

[handwritten: N+P £100. Oct 4th 91.]

The mortgagor's valuation fee

This is a check on the value of the house on behalf of whoever is giving you the mortgage. You pay. Sometimes you commission it, but building societies commission it themselves and only recently even allowed you to see it. Their decision on what proportion of the purchase price to offer you is based on it. Their view is that it is totally non-committal and if you want a proper survey you ought to get your own. The fees, however, are modest: on a property costing £10,000 you would pay £21 plus VAT; on one costing £25,000 you would pay £46 plus VAT.

Your surveyor's fee

This is your survey, which again you pay for, to check the structural soundness of the house or flat and reveal any serious work which has to be done, or defects like dry-rot, bad wiring, leaky roof, etc.

It is important to get a qualified surveyor. He will belong to either The Royal Institution of Chartered Surveyors (FRICS or ARICS), or The Incorporated Society of Valuers and Auctioneers

(FIAS or AIAS). These organisations will give you names of members in your area.

It is also important, as there is no fixed scale of fees, to negotiate with him first of all on the type of report you need and the fee he will expect. The report can be oral or written. It might take in specialist tests for damp, woodworm or dry rot. (These, done by specialists firms, are usually free.) Or tests of the wiring or gas installations or drains (not free). If the previous owners have had work carried out and possess guarantees, it saves time and money because your surveyor can take these into account and they can usually be transferred to you if you buy the place.

Getting this survey is an insurance for yourself. It is essential on an old house. But even with a new house, if it is on a National House Builders Council (NHBC) guarantee, you need an independent survey before you can invoke the guarantee.

Land Registry fees

In many areas (including most urban areas) property (or the land it stands on) is compulsorily registered at the Land Registry — a government department.

When registered property changes hands there is a charge for changing the register. It is on a fixed scale and comes to about ¼% of the price. As the advantage of a registered property is that it gives you a guarantee of ownership, there is less work involved for your solicitor transferring ownership and therefore he should charge you less (see below). At one time you could register property voluntarily, but this option has been temporarily suspended because of government spending cuts.

Stamp duty

This is a tax on house sales of houses above a certain price. Noises are made from time to time to abolish it, but all that has happened so far is that it is now payable on anything over £25,000.

The scale goes up from ½% of the price on houses between £25,001 — £30,000 to 2% on houses costing above £40,000.

Conveyancing costs

These are all the costs involved in transferring ownership from one person to another. The cost includes searches, titles, drawing up the contract and preparing all the documents. Most people use a solicitor. We always have. In Scotland you have to.

However there has been a revolt against the solicitor's monopoly and it is not illegal in England and Wales and Ulster to use firms of conveyancers who are not qualified solicitors and who do the job more cheaply. There are also some thorough and persistent individuals who do it for themselves, even cheaper (if you don't cost your own time).

a. Your solicitor's charges. There used to be a fixed scale but in 1973 this was abolished and you are now charged on the basis of time taken/value of house/difficulties encountered/speed required, etc. If the cost worries you ask for an estimate of the fee in advance. It is usually in the region of 1% of the purchase price plus VAT.

To find a solicitor, you can either ask friends or business colleagues to recommend someone, or go to the Citizen's Advice Bureau or the public library and pick a name from the local law list.

b. Solicitor's charges for the mortgage deed. This is for whoever is lending you the money. There is a rate agreed between the building societies and the Law Society for this job which should more or less apply to any mortgage deed. If the same solicitor draws up the mortgage deed and does the conveyancing for you, the scale of fees is lower. It is based on the actual sum lent. Allow about £35 plus VAT on a mortgage of £5,000, and £75 on a mortgage of £25,000 if the same solicitor is doing both conveyancing and the deed. Allow 60% more if not.

House-hunting 3

'Elle a des idées au dessous de sa gare'
TERENCE RATTIGAN, French without Tears.

House-hunting without tears is possible — if you have some idea what you're looking for. In other words if you have already come to some conclusions about price, area and type of house before you set out to look at anything at all. There are three decisions you have to make before you even look at an ad or speak to an estate agent.

Decide on your price range

This is not really a decision. It is a fact of life. In the previous chapter we have discussed how much you are likely to be able to borrow, how much extra you'll need just to buy a place. Keep these figures in mind.

Many prudent people never look at anything above their fixed price range because, they say, it makes them moody, dissatisfied with their lot in life and they lose the ability to see the good points in what they can afford. But don't be too rigid. There are many others around today who balked at the final £250* on an asking price ten years ago, lost a good house, and now wonder why they drew such a firm line. Inflation is going to continue and its effects on mortgage repayments is wholly beneficial in that the payments, in real terms, get smaller!

Decide on the area

Think in general terms. Rural solitude — or busy community complete with nosy neighbours and obligations to produce cakes, old clothes, crafts or just your personal presence? Big city life — or the leafy peace of the suburbs? If you can make up your mind

*The £250 of ten years ago is the equivalent of about £2,000 in house-price terms today.

SETTING UP HOME

on the general environment you want, you can relate this to where you've got to be and what you can afford.

Work is the factor that ties most people to one place or another. The more convenient it is to get to work the more time you have for all the other things you want to do. A long journey every day is tiring at best, but absolute hell when anything interrupts the routine — snow on the roads, rail strikes, go-slows or bus cancellations. Public transport is also expensive, and you have no control over the way fares go up.

The decision becomes more complicated if two of you are working. Unless you come from a long-line of much separated naval couples with an inherited stoicism which makes separations bearable, if not enjoyable, one or other of you usually has to compromise. One has the quick easy journey, the other struggles across country — or changes his or her job.

Having checked out work journeys, you are in a position to pinpoint where you might look. At this stage, get a big map and mark the areas on it. Plan routes to work or to stations. If you are aiming for a place in a town or city, get a street-map and do the same thing.

Everyone (almost) needs friends nearby — or if you have to settle in some strange place, people around who could be friends. Mixed communities are wonderful in theory, but not if you are the only people under thirty for miles.

If you choose a very conveniently placed pad in London (or Oxford, or Edinburgh, or any big city people find themselves drawn to from time to time) your home will become a staging post for all your friends. Be prepared!

Family and relations. Some of us wish to live nearer our families than others. This depends entirely on how knit-up you are with your home environment.

Shops. However much you may dislike shopping, it has to be done — and it goes on having to be done. It's well worth checking out the shopping in any area before you decide to live there.

For example, if you want to do a big once-a-week raid on a supermarket and take advantage of lower prices — make sure there is a supermarket you like within range. Make sure also you can park and load, etc. Carrying a week's shopping on public transport is not fun.

If you prefer just getting what you want when you need it, shops that don't open until after you've gone to work and are closed when you come back are useless. Many shops in small market towns and villages still operate like this, but the shop which stays open very late is appearing gradually outside the inner cities and we must all hope the Indian families who are so much more flexible and business-like in their approach to shop-keeping, prosper and open shops in more places.

Amenities. By this we mean good places to walk, sporting facilities, theatres and art galleries — activities generally. Some areas are better than others for different things. One may have an active tennis club, another a wonderful swimming pool complex. There are colleges of further education which hum with courses you'd like to take, others which stick to keep fit and upholstery for geriatrics. If a place has amenities for doing something you like, there are obviously people around with similar interests and therefore possible friends. The local public library is a good place to start enquiring about things run by the local authority. They may also know about privately-run clubs as well.

Local authority plans. Many authorities have what they call their development plans which schedule areas for further development, no development, offices, industrial or housing estates. When you buy a property, part of the conveyancing work you pay for is to check that there are no plans which will affect your ownership of that particular property. But the whole area may be subtly altered by plans which don't directly affect your home — a new industrial estate, a motorway, a conference centre, school, hospital or even a gravel pit.

You can talk with the area planning officer at the local authority quite informally. It is best to telephone first and arrange an appointment.

Transport. You must obviously be able to get to work. What about the shops, the amenities, your friends? If you have no car you have to make sure most things are within walking distance — or bicycling distance (and get yourself one). Because to rely on buses when schedules may be cut, is to put your life into a terrible straitjacket. It is one thing to live to a time-table to get to and from work on time, it is quite another to have to plan all the rest of your life around time-tables.

You can check on British Rail plans from the regional offices who will tell you what is public knowledge, but not secret or undecided options. Bus companies will also tell you current

SETTING UP HOME

plans. If you do have a car, motor-bike or moped, it is worth checking parking regulations in the area. Where parking is restricted or about to be, you may find you have to invest in a parking permit. Ask the local authority planning department.

Having made all these enquiries and marked your map, deleting some possibilities and adding others, the next step, if possible, is to wander around any possible areas, just getting the feel of them, map to hand. See which particular places make you feel most at home.

Decide on what type of house or flat

When you know what price you can afford and which areas you want to look in, the type of place you are looking for begins to emerge of its own accord.

Don't be depressed if it bears very little resemblance to your dream house. Very few of us get our dream places first go. For instance, you will be able to see what sort of place exists in your chosen area — new estate-built house, Victorian terrace, purpose-built flat, converted flat, thirties semi, or tiny cottage.

If you are desperate to get into one particular area you may have to sacrifice all sorts of other needs to get there. But there is an old adage which says better the worst house in the best street, than the best house in the worst street. You can do a lot to transform some pretty unpromising toe-holds as the way New Yorkers tackle their tiny Manhattan apartments shows. But single-handed there isn't a lot you can do to upgrade a whole neighbourhood.

If you are competent at D-I-Y or even just good with your hands and practical, you can take on and enjoy quite different property from people who can really only attempt some of the things we list in Chapter 13. You can take on places that would simply cost other people too much to put right. You are at an advantage because you can snap up places that the less practical people would need time to think about.

If you have sorted some of these questions out in your mind before you actually start looking at places, you'll save a lot of time. You'll be able to reject a great deal of what you are told will be perfect for you (by the estate agent) without even looking at it. You'll be able to recognise and act quickly on a good prospect.

Starting the hunt

In the market for what the trade calls 'starter homes' there is always pressure. £200,000 houses may be languishing unwanted, but the reasonable, affordable places get snapped up. You want to get the best one possible for you, because that is the one that you are going to find most easy and profitable to sell when the time comes. So you want to hear about everything suitable for you that's on the market at the moment. Luckily for you all this information is free.

1. Contact all the estate agents who deal in the area. Try and find someone responsive in each agent's office to talk to about what you want. They may have useful advice to give about prices, areas, etc. Don't limit yourself to the big agents; go round the small ones. They have more incentive to be interested in you. You find the agents operating from ads in the local press, boards on local houses and personal recommendation.

As a buyer you will pay the agent nothing unless you specifically commission him to find you something in which case he will expect an agreed percentage of the purchase price. Most people prefer to do without this extra expense, and just get the agents' standard lists of property within (and often way outside) their price range.

You must be zealous to get anything out of estate agents. To get ahead of the field, don't wait for the lists to arrive by post, telephone once a week or more often. If you make a nuisance of yourself, they often tell you of somewhere, just to get you off the line.

People do not have to have any qualifications to set up as an estate agent. However there are several professional bodies which lay down charges, codes of conduct, etc. If the partners belong to one of them you have a better guarantee that your business will be handled professionally and some come-back if it is not. These bodies are: The Royal Institution of Chartered Surveyors (FRICS or ARICS); The Incorporated Society of Valuers and Auctioneers (FSVA or ASVA); The Rating and Valuing Association (FRVA); The National Association of Estate Agents (MNAEA).

2. Just starting up are the computer-based introductory agencies like Homeline in London. The firms build up a list which the seller pays to get on. Buyers phone in their needs and are sent a selection of suitable properties from the list, free.

3. Ads in local and national papers. With cheaper property, many people like to save the estate agent's fee by advertising themselves. The local papers are often a good hunting ground.

SETTING UP HOME

But remember that individuals have not perhaps had a lot of experience of selling their houses/flats and the transaction can all too easily get bogged down because there isn't an agent to push it along. You need to be very businesslike, if not pushy, to get the sale through.

National papers — like *The Sunday Times*, *Observer* and *The Times* — have house ads put in by owners as do the specialist weekly publications *Dalton's Weekly* and *Exchange and Mart*.

4. Ads for new estate houses. Builders and developers sometimes put their own advertisements in local papers to sell new houses. If you want a new house, follow up these ads — not just for the estate advertised, but for further particulars of the developer's plans elsewhere as well.

There are specialist publications about new houses which come out monthly: *House-buyer*, *Buying Your Home* and *Homefinder*.

Planning departments of local authorities would also be able to tell you who has received planning permission to start work on an estate in the near future.

5. Ask around. Ask friends in the area of course. But also try to pick up local gossip. Local people in the country often know of places which are coming up for sale. They certainly know who the big landowners are who just might have an empty cottage or flat. Time spent 'researching' in the pub is often well spent.

6. The personal approach. If there is a particular house, street, block of flats, or estate where you would really like to live and nothing seems to be for sale, there is no harm in approaching the owners personally and enquiring whether they might consider selling. We often have duplicated letters through our letter boxes, asking if we would think of selling all or part of our houses. There's usually a quick run-through of the good qualities of the person wanting the place, financial reliability, etc, as well. When it comes to putting a price on the place you want, make a generous offer — at least what an estate agent would suggest — possibly a little more so it is not worth the owner's while to put it on the market themselves.

Check-list for the house-hunter

1. Your kit — before you do anything else, equip yourself with:
    a notebook
    a steel tape, 30ft (10m) with inches and centimetres marked
    pencils or biros

a penknife
a compass
a torch

In the back of the notebook, write down vital statistics which for the house-hunter are all the measurements of their own pictures, furniture or hi-fi that MUST fit in. You could also write in some standard sizes to help you see, for instance, whether the double bedroom will really take your double bed.

Take this kit around with you to every place you look at and write in the particulars of each.

2. You know the price of the place. Now you need to find out the running costs: rates, heating costs (and how these work — partial, full, all day, just evenings, etc.), hot water system. In a flat there may be a service charge, etc.

3. Services. Whether there is electricity, gas, water or mains? What sort of drains? Where the meters are. The fuse boxes. Whether chimneys work — or would have to be unblocked. If oil, solid fuels or wood are used what are the storage arrangements?

4. General structure. Your surveyor will do a full report if you are in any doubt, but when you go around you should look out for:

Roof — tiles/slates missing, chimneys leaning.

Gutters and down-pipes — not broken, no damp patches visible on walls by them.

External walls — cracks in the fabric, inside or outside, mortar in joints crumbling or missing, are there signs of a damp-proof course about 6in (15cm) above ground?

External woodwork — doors, porch if any and windows, whether well painted or not, whether windows all open properly.

Internal signs of damp — stains on walls and ceilings inside.

Condition of floorboards and skirtings — especially in basements, ground-floors without cellars and attics. (Jump on them to see how firm they are.) If damp they may have wet rot. If dry and powdery, dry rot. Stab with your penknife, and if wood is rotten it will go in.

Walls and ceilings in good condition? No cracks in the plaster or bumpy crumbling areas?

Condition of electric points and wiring, i.e. existence of old points, surface wiring and not taking 13-amp square pin plugs is a bad sign.

SETTING UP HOME

5. Note the aspect of the outside — the compass comes in here to tell you if the place faces south or west or whatever. Then, you can guess how sunny it is. Indoors too — when will the different rooms get the sun? At the same time note privacy (or not), noise levels, etc.

6. Ignore all decorations and owner's furniture, flying ducks and frilly curtains — unless you like them. Decoration is the easiest thing to remedy. But notice floors. Good quality, pleasant flooring is a bonus because it can be expensive to change.

7. Kitchens and bathrooms which look and work well are also a bonus because they too are expensive to alter.

8. Storage. Is there any built-in already and is it the right size? Can you visualise where you will store everything eventually? Remember large possessions like skis or suitcases you will not need all the time. Where will you put coats, macs, shopping trolleys, bikes?

9. In a flat, check the ventilation out from the kitchen and bathroom and the intrusion of other people's noise, cooking smells, etc., into the flat.

10. In a newly-built house — is it under the NHBC ten year guarantee? What plans exist for 'finishing' the estate? Is any planting to be done or landscaping?

Steps to take to buy a place

These apply to England and Wales only. There are slightly different formalities in Scotland. Also if you buy at auction or by tender. We discuss these later.

Make your offer

Tell the owner or estate agent the amount you are prepared to offer — *subject to contract*. This can be done orally or by letter. And the proviso covers you if, for some reason, you can't go forward with the purchase — the survey may reveal some terrible defect. You also have to decide whether to include the price of any fittings or carpets the owner wishes to sell in the price (better for the mortgage calculations) or as a separate deal (better for stamp duty, estate agent fees, etc.).

If your offer is accepted, the estate agent will ask you for the name and address of your solicitor or whoever is doing the conveyancing and a small deposit to show you are serious. A small amount — £50 or £100 is often enough and should be paid to the estate agent or seller's solicitor with a cheque endorsed on the back 'as stakeholder'. You need a receipt saying it has been received, is being held as stakeholder and that the offer is subject to contract and survey.

Nothing is binding to either party at this stage. Until the contracts have been exchanged the seller can accept a higher offer or you can withdraw. It is nice if after your offer has been accepted the seller considers his house/flat 'under offer' and no-one else makes a better bid.

Sometimes the seller is under pressure to sell quickly and there is a lot of interest, so to protect himself his solicitor sends contracts out to several people and the one who returns the contract first gets the property.

Get your survey in hand if necessary

Decide how full a survey you need (see page 24). If you are getting your own survey, ask the surveyor to estimate how much it will cost to put the place into good structural repair. If it is a buyer's market, you may be able to get the price reduced. A surveyor's report is a valid reason for breaking off negotiations and/or cancelling your offer.

Get your mortgage arrangements moving

The sort of mortgage you are aiming for should have been sorted out in principle with bank, building society, broker or whoever might lend you the money before you start hunting. Now you notify them that you have found somewhere and you wish to apply for a mortgage and would they arrange to have their valuation survey done.

(If the market is very competitive, and you lose the house/flat before the surveyor for this survey has been round, you can cancel him: otherwise, whatever the outcome, you have to pay.)

Start drafting the contract

This is your solicitor's/conveyancer's job — or yours if you are doing it yourself.

It is the basis of the document by which the property will become yours. The seller's solicitor sends yours a draft contract and yours makes all enquiries necessary to make sure there is no reason why you should not buy and he alters the draft if necessary. It will show:

Property: Address and how it is shown on an attached plan.
Vendor: Name.
Price: Whatever has been agreed.
Deposit: Usually 10% and when it is to be paid.
Completion: End of sale when house/flat is yours and how long it will take.
Title: Where and how it is registered. (If at the Land Registry this cuts down much work and should cut down the solicitor's charges by as much as 30%.)
Roads: Whether the adjoining roads are maintained at public or private expense.
Planning: How area is zoned and what proposals there are for redevelopment. These are the 'Searches'.
Drainage: Description of main and rain-water drainage.
Services: Whether water, gas, electricity supplies or drainage cross other people's property, and if there are any conditions attached.
Restrictive covenants: Whether there are any.
Outgoings: Sums you have to pay out — e.g. rates.
Insurance: When it will be liable.
Mortgage: Details.

You will have had to decide, if there are two of you involved, how you are going to work out the joint ownership. Joint tenancy is the usual form for husband and wife. Neither can sell without the other's agreement. If one dies, the other inherits his share automatically. Tenancy in common is more like co-ownership, as each can dispose of his share as he/she thinks fit during lifetime or by will.

Time taken varies. If the searches are done in the normal line of duty by local authorities, they can take four or five weeks — even longer. If you pay the solicitor to spend his valuable time (or one of his minion's time) searching, it can take a day, or less. Alterations are agreed by the contracts to-ing and fro-ing between solicitors, so this can also take time. Four to eight weeks seems normal.

Exchanging the contracts

You and the seller each receive identical copies of the contract once it has been agreed between the solicitors. You each sign your copy. You, as buyer, have to hand over your deposit of 10% of the purchase price, less anything you gave initially. You are now bound as is the seller.

Completion day
You pay over the money and receive in exchange the deeds of the house and the conveyancing document. (Actually the deeds usually go straight off to whoever is lending you the money.) The time between the exchange of contracts and completion is taken with sorting out your mortgage, getting the money etc. You will not only have to pay the remaining 90% of the purchase price, but also the Land Registry fee and the stamp duty if any, probably also the solicitor. Completion day is also the day the keys and documents about the house (guarantees, etc.) are handed over to you and you could in theory move in.

Buying a house at auction

If you are the successful bidder at an auction, you sign a memorandum of contract immediately and pay over your 10% deposit. This is as binding as an exchange of contracts and you have usually twenty-eight days to sort out everything before completion day.

This means that if you need a survey it has to have been completed before the auction. You also have to be sure you can get the mortgage!

The estate agents/auctioneers prepare a full brochure about the property they are about to auction. Send a copy of this to your solicitors so they can carry out the enquiries and searches before the day of the auction. Sometimes places are sold before being auctioned. If the particulars say 'by order of the executors' the place will go to auction because the purpose of auctioning it is to ensure that a proper price has been achieved. If there is a phrase like 'unless previously sold' it means that the property is open to offers and you would be wise to make one. Otherwise it may get sold before the auction without your knowing.

Buying by tender

This is like an auction but instead of going along and bidding, you send your offer plus a cheque for 10% deposit along to the agent handling it by a specific date. The best offer gets the property.

SETTING UP HOME

The procedure for buying in Scotland

There are several differences between the procedures in England and Wales and those in Scotland. In some ways we can't help feeling the Scottish one makes more sense.*

1. Solicitors are active as well as estate agents in dealing in property. There are no boards put up, so you rely on contacting estate agents, solicitors' offices or solicitors' joint property centres in main shopping areas. Or look at the advertisements in local papers and bigger ones like *The Scotsman* and *The Glasgow Herald*.

2. You have to deal through solicitors. No chance of doing your own conveyancing.

3. If you want to make an offer, you first get your solicitor to ring the seller's solicitor to tell him 'to note your interest'. This means the house will not be sold without you being given a chance to make an offer.

4. You make a formal offer through your solicitor when you have had a survey and got the mortgage fixed in principle. This offer is really equivalent to the draft contract. But it includes a date for completion and offer for any furniture or fittings in the sale.

5. If your offer is accepted, the terms of the offer are negotiated between the solicitors, and three or four days later a final letter is sent to your solicitor, which concludes the bargain. You are now committed and so is the seller.

6. Completion day is when the money and the keys are handed over.

*For more details get a free booklet *Buying or Selling a House?* from the Law Society of Scotland (see page 157).

Getting the basics right 4

The advantage of having had a proper survey before you buy your house or flat is that you then know exactly what the state of the fabric is — if there is anything that needs doing urgently and/or that it is free from such defects as dry rot, sinking foundations or badly leaking roof.

This chapter is about how to keep the fabric in good order together with some ideas about how you can improve it, so that your home not only keeps you more comfortable but also has a greater re-sale value.

The fabric

Roof and chimneys

These are particularly vulnerable and tend to get forgotten until something serious happens. Chimneys can be dangerous and a source of damp if pointing between bricks or stones is eroded, particularly if carrying a television aerial. The junction between roof slates or tiles and chimney stacks is a common source of leaks. Slipped tiles and slates may not show up from outside, so a roof hatch is vital to let you check from inside, insulate, get at the cold water storage tank, treat roof timbers, store trunks, etc.

Walls

Walls do two jobs: they keep out the weather and keep out the cold. Also, the 'drier' the wall, the better it insulates. Two things keep it dry. The most important is the damp-proof course (DPC) which prevents damp from travelling upwards from the ground. Your survey should tell you of the existence and condition of the DPC. If there isn't one, the grants department at your local authority can tell you if you are eligible for a grant to put one in and recommend reliable specialist firms who could do it. These firms will survey your property free and it is worth getting a range of different opinions as well as prices. You can help the situation by keeping earth clear of all air-bricks and avoid bridging any existing DPC. Paving surrounding the house should be gently sloped to carry water away from rather than towards it.

Thick 13ins (33cm) brick and 18ins (46cm) stone walls will dry out naturally and seldom if ever allow the damp to penetrate to the inner surface of the walls. You are not so safe with 9in (23cm) brick walls which, even while not actually letting the damp through, can absorb enough to be very cold and so encourage condensation which chills the house. This is why keeping walls in good repair and re-pointing when necessary is important. You can increase effectiveness by brushing with a colourless silicone like Synthasil. (Although this acts like a mackintosh to prevent rain penetrating, being permeable, it allows the walls to breathe and any residual damp to escape. For the same reason if you paint walls, make sure you use a paint that is permeable (such as ICI's Weathershield).) Tile and slate hanging and weather-boarding are all traditional ways of improving the wall's water shedding and insulating functions, and so are well worth keeping in good repair.

Cavity walls (two layers of brick) have been widely used since 1919 as a means of preventing rain penetration and are more effective than solid walls. Their insulation potential is discussed below.

Foundations

If the survey throws any doubt about soundness of foundations, don't buy. If you want to build on top of an existing single storey flat-roofed extension get the surveyor to check that its foundations and walls are adequate to meet the building regulations' requirements for the extra load.

Windows and doors

Keep in good order by regular painting. If using a contractor, insist in writing for a written confirmation stating that work is carried out entirely to manufacturer's recommendations as to priming, undercoats, top coats etc. and that all paints used come from the same manufacturer. For example, ICI recommend, and JL finds it pays off, for outside woodwork to be given two top gloss coats. New timber can be treated more cheaply and with less skill with tinted preservative treatments which range from pure black to pure white through many colours. It is better to paint woodwork after a dry spell when the wood is not swollen with rain. Bolting doors and casement windows top and bottom will help stop them warping and reduce draughts. In old houses it is often better to provide double-glazing rather than replace frail existing windows which are in period and character with the house. Far too many old houses and cottages are spoilt by inappropriate aluminium and timber replacement windows — and also devalued in price.

Floors
Suspended wood floors (with earth directly below them) are particularly vulnerable to rot and worm. If there is no guarantee, get a specialist firm to lift the boards and spray preservative fluid underneath and get their guarantee. (Don't get it done by a builder, however good, because he can't give you a foolproof guarantee.) Make sure all airbricks are clear and there are enough of them to provide good cross ventilation under the floor. If you are advised to remove the floor (because of serious rot), replace it with a concrete one incorporating a damp-proof bituminous membrane, (not a plastic sheet). For better insulation, if there is sufficient depth include an inch of polystyrene rigid panel below the two-inch topping screed.

An existing concrete floor should be checked for damp (by the surveyor) as this will affect what you can safely lay as flooring. The various Building Centres will recommend products for sealing concrete floors which don't have damp-proof membranes.

Drains
In town, foul (household waste) drains run to a main sewer in the road and have man-holes with removable covers at changes of direction which provide access for rodding in case of blockages. You are responsible for your drains up to their junction with the main sewer.

In the country, if there is no mains drainage, there should be either a cess-pit which will need periodic emptying, (either the local authority or a private firm will do this for a fee) or a septic

Services

SETTING UP HOME

tank, which unless over used (too much foaming detergent) can be self-regulating over a number of years without attention.

Town rain water gets carried away by mains surface-water drains. In the country it usually runs from the down pipes underground to soak-aways some distance from the house and percolates into the ground from there.

Have gutters and down pipes checked as inconspicuous leaks and blockages can create damp patches on walls and start timbers rotting.

No new connections should be made to the drainage system without informing the local authority.

Water

Most houses, except for isolated farms and cottages, will be supplied with mains water. The water authority brings the supply pipe along under the road or across nearby fields and, if not connected, the householder is responsible for connecting the supply to his own property. (This has to be in approved piping and to an approved depth to avoid contamination and freezing.) If your present connecting pipe is lead you would be wise to replace it as soon as possible.

Mains water enters the house with a stop-cock at its point of entry. One branch runs to the kitchen sink which should have its own stop-cock. Another will run up the house to feed the cold water storage tank, if there is one. (It may be in the roof space, or on top of the hot-water cylinder in an airing cupboard.) This tank provides cold water to baths, showers, basins and WCs as well as to the hot water cylinder. (It needs to be a good 3ft (100cm) above a showerhead to give sufficient pressure.) You should make sure it has a tight-fitting lid over it to keep out insects, birds and mice etc. Some property runs all its water services from the mains only.

Find out whether the water is hard. If so, set hot water thermostats to no higher than 140°F to discourage the build up of scale on immersion heaters and in pipes. Run washing machines on lower settings and use Calgon (not soda) to soften water for baths and washing clothes.

If you have well water, the local authority will test it for you to see if it is safe to drink.

Electricity

All but the most remote cottages are connected to mains

electricity these days. All wiring up to the meter-box is the electricity authority's responsibility. If the present cable is inadequate for the amount of equipment you plan to use and a larger one is needed, then the authority will charge you for the new installation. The same would apply if you were making a first-time connection to a cottage which has mains electricity running nearby but has never been connected up.

If no space or water-heating uses off-peak power there will be one single meter which will clock up all power used for lighting, heating and cooking. If there are night storage heaters there will be either an additional off-peak meter for these running on Tariff E, giving an eight-hour overnight charge, or there will be a single meter running on Day/Night Tariff — Economy 7. This has a seven-hour charging period for heaters when it will run any other equipment switched on at the same cheap rate.

When adding power points make them doubles rather than singles because all you will be paying for extra is the price of the slightly larger box. It is better to have too many power points than too few, but check that the present power supply can take them. As an average allow four doubles in a living room, three in dining rooms and studies, two in bedrooms, four in kitchens and three in utility rooms.

If you are out all day, consider an external meter.

All electrical authorities have a contract department who will carry out domestic installations and check over the existing system for safety, at a charge. If you go to an outside firm, demand in writing a written confirmation that all work will be carried out to The Institute of Electrical Engineers' specifications. Your electricity board showroom will have a list of electricians whose work is approved by them.

Gas
There is only one domestic tariff, and the standard size pipe supplying gas from the mains to the domestic meter can cope with any demands made on it. The Gas Board will check your installation and supply, and will charge you for this. All central-heating boilers and water heaters should be checked regularly once a year, not only for safety but for greatest efficiency in operation. External meters are now standard in new property. When relaying mains and connections for old property on a

whole road external meters are fitted automatically whenever it is suitable. If you want an external meter, check whether this is due to happen to your road in the near future as you will get your external meter free. Otherwise the charge will be between £100 and £200. As we write, where houses have no gas supply the Gas Board will not make new connections farther than twenty-three metres from the main supply. However virtually all equipment run on mains gas can be bought with adapted burners to run off bottled gas. You will find suppliers in the Yellow Pages and your local Gas Board salesroom will know who operates locally. Bottled gas is more expensive than mains gas but some 10% cheaper than oil.

Insulation

Think about insulation before heating, with the prime object of providing comfort rather than warmth. Heat input can be reduced to a minimum if effective insulation and efficient controls are installed. So if there is no existing installation or what exists seems inadequate, insulate first; you will then be able to install a smaller and cheaper system than you would in the house as it stands, or find that the apparently inadequate system is now adequate.

Aim to turn your house into a tea-cosy without spending the earth. You can't stop heat escaping completely; the object is to slow it down as much as possible. Many effective forms of insulation are easy to install yourself. These are the ones to go for. (Even if you keep fuel bills and weather records to prove its amazing effectiveness, it may at some future date be hard to persuade a potential buyer that the thousands you have spent on the best bespoke double-glazing make your house worth that much more than its neighbour.)

A high level of insulation and sophisticated controls can considerably reduce the size, and therefore the installation cost, as well as the running costs of your heating system. So insulate first and make sure your installer takes this into account. JL found she was able to reduce her boiler size by 25% simply by doubling the depth of her roof insulation and setting her thermostats to give a continuous temperature of 63°F instead of at 68°F at set periods as she had formerly.

Continuous heating even at a low temperature allows solid structures to charge with heat and by reflecting it back into the rooms makes the occupants feel comfortably warm, whereas with high air temperatures created for short periods only, the structure does not have time to charge up and so draws heat from the people in the room who as a result feel cold and uncomfortable even though the air is itself very warm. Highly insulated surfaces, because they do not absorb heat, reflect back any heat input to the room and can maintain a comfortable environment even when the heating system comes on for limited periods.

Roof

Start here first, as heat rises. Before insulating your roof space be sure to treat the timbers first against rot as insulation materials can inhibit ventilation and damp still air provides ideal conditions for dry rot.

If no felt or boarding exists below slates or tiles, staple a thick polystyrene sheet on to the underside of the rafters to prevent cold draughts, but leave a few little gaps for ventilation.

Warm air from rooms below carries with it damp in the form of water vapour which can start rot if it becomes trapped in roof timbers. So either paint the bedroom ceilings with an impermeable oil-based paint, undercoat would do, or lay sheets of thin polythene over the ceiling joists and down into the spaces between, before you infill to the top of the joists with glass or mineral quilt. Loose fill is cheaper but blows about and is unbelievably difficult to move if changes in the roof are made later. If you lay chipboard on the ceiling joists to make storage easier, you improve the insulation even further. Don't forget, if the cold water storage tank is in the roof to insulate *over* it, never under it and wrap any pipes generously as the better insulated the bedroom ceilings the less warmth escapes upwards, so the more vulnerable they become.

Sloping roofs are best lined on the underside with foam or foil-backed plaster board or T & G boarding set on battens with panels of insulation between. Pumping foam or mineral wool down between the ceiling joists is an alternative but it is argued

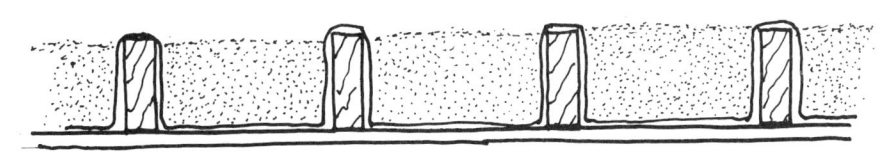

Figure 1. *Insulating Your Roof*. Follow the line of the ceiling except to go over the cold water storage tank to stop it freezing. You should paint your ceilings with an oil-bound impermeable paint or run plastic sheet over the joists and down into the gaps between before packing in the insulation.

that this could trap damp air and start up rot. Flat roofs can be treated as sloping ones but the cheapest answer is to simply lay large 2ins (5cms) thick panels of polystyrene on top of the existing roof surface.

Walls

First get them dry, since wet walls are cold walls (see Fabric). Cavity walls can be filled, and although a little more expensive, blown mineral wool and polystyrene bead systems have several advantages over urea formaldehyde foam ones (which are now no longer used in the U.S.A. and Canada because of the toxic fumes produced during installation). Solid walls can be lined on the inside with wall-to-wall, floor-to-ceiling cupboards and bookshelves to provide buffers against heat loss, or lined with finishes as under ceilings.

Windows

Check whether there are shutters nailed back in the side panels or, in the case of sash windows, sometimes in the panel beneath. If so, use them. Next draught strip. Modern foam strip encased in a white plastic sheath is easy to apply, and lasts for a long time without looking tatty. Openable double-glazing needs to be very substantial to be effective, which tends to make it expensive. At this stage in your property-owning career decide which windows are not needed for ventilation during the winter and fit an unobtrusive fixed double-glazing system like Grippa-Frame which, if fitted with acrylic sheet or Perspex instead of glass, can be easily and safely dismantled in the summer if necessary. Even net curtains thickly gathered make a useful contribution, as do blinds. Drawing all curtains at night is important, and if they are generous in size with aluminium-coated (Milium) linings they will be doubly effective.

Doors

Whether they are front doors, back doors or French ones they should be draught-stripped like windows and fitted with a draught-excluding threshold strip such as Duraflex. Put an inside flap on your letter-box and double-glaze larger glass door panels with unobtrusive Grippa-frame. Glazed porches and inner glazed doors in halls provide useful airlocks, so do greenhouses and conservatories outside kitchen and French windows or sliding doors.

Floors

Ensure first that concrete floors are dry (see Fabric). Then lay aluminium foil beneath insulation-backed vinyl sheeting, foam-backed carpet or thick rush or coir matting. On timber floors seal them first against draughts with sheets of hardboard and then flooring as above.

The heating

As all fuel prices rise inexorably and supplies are affected by shortages, strikes and sometimes bad weather, it is hard to decide on what kind of heating to choose on a best-buy principle. We think that it is more sensible to aim for flexibility, both in the system you install and the fuels you use. The first step is to check on what fuels are available — in the house and in the area.

The fuels

Electricity — Electricity is virtually maintenance-free and allows for an easy inexpensive installation. Running costs, though high, can be reduced by super insulation and sophisticated time and temperature controls. Night storage systems are becoming increasingly efficient as well as neat looking and provide the cheapest form of electric space and water heating.

Gas — Gas is currently the cheapest fuel, demanding little maintenance. It is also extremely flexible in use. Most equipment is available for use with either conventional or balanced flues; existing brick flues can be used provided they are suitably lined. Pre-fabricated conventional flues with insulated outer skins can run up through the house in cupboards etc. to a roof terminal or be attached to an outside wall. All appliances using conventional flues draw air from the room they are in and require for safety permanent ventilation. Balanced flues which can be pushed through any outside wall at a point sufficiently distant from surrounding windows etc. draw fresh air in for combustion from the outside as well as emitting the gases formed from combustion, which means that the appliance connected to it does not draw air from the room and no permanent ventilation is needed.

Bottled gas — Large scale cylinders are available when bottled gas is used for central heating but suppliers demand space for their delivery lorry to park off the road. Bottled gas can be useful when your house is above the road and oil would have to be pumped up from the storage tank at road level. The gas rises naturally up from the tank to the house on demand.

Oil — Oil is almost as expensive as electricity as we write. As it is almost as automatic as gas it can be useful in a topping-up role when wood or solid fuel is in general use, but refuelling is inconvenient. Have the largest tank available as supplies always seem to get difficult when the weather is at its worst and you have run out. Bulk buying gives a cheaper rate too. Shop around to get the best terms; many suppliers offer a useful maintenance service and oil boilers need servicing twice a year. Local suppliers will be found in the Yellow Pages.

Avoid paraffin stoves as they produce a gallon of water (in vapour form) for every gallon of oil burnt, which aggravates any existing dampness.

Solid fuel — Coal, smokeless fuel, anthracite, wood, peat, dry rubbish. Many solid fuel room heaters and boilers (particularly those using anthracite) will now stay in for twenty-four hours and some even for a weekend. Before long in low energy houses, this will be extended to a whole week. Solid fuel is valuable because appliances using it burn continuously rather than on/off. This charges the whole fabric of the surrounding walls and floor with warmth so that rooms are comfortable at comparatively low temperatures. The best modern appliances can give efficiencies up to 70% and so match the best of oil and gas appliances and it is well worth shopping around for them. The Building Centre in London has a showroom run by the Solid Fuel Advisory Service — which can give you details of their regional offices. Generous dry storage is vital, a proportion of it at least, close by or within the house. Increasing use of solid fuel in conjunction with more expensive topping-up fuels is being encouraged by forward-looking heating consultants and the Solid Fuel Advisory Service is promoting it in its Link System. The most flexible appliances are those which will burn every sort of solid fuel so that you can use what is most conveniently available at any given time. Check whether you live in a smokeless zone where only smokeless fuels are permitted to be burnt although smoke-eater appliances are available which burn ordinary bituminous coal and then cleverly consume the resulting fumes to provide further heat.

Ambient Energy — This is the energy drawn directly from natural sources — wind for windmills, rushing streams for mill wheels, sun for solar panels and the low temperature warmth in the earth, air and even rivers for heat pumps. It is the last which turns a large amount of low temperature heat into a small amount of high temperature heat — like a refrigerator in reverse — which we feel first home buyers might find worth looking into. There are models on the market which can provide both space and water heating for a small house running either radiators or warm air systems, at prices roughly competitive with other installations. Solar panels cannot yet cope with full house heating in this country but can be useful to boost a hot water supply. However, at this stage in your property-owning career, money is usually better invested in insulation and controls than on ambient energy systems. Nevertheless, things are beginning to move fast in this field and by the time you are into your second house there may well be any number of well-proved possibilities open to you.

Heating systems — what to do if they are adequate

Basically, all you have to do is to ensure they are maintained! And, where possible, consider how to introduce more flexibility or alternative fuel.

a. Gas-fired hot-water central heating: get boiler serviced once a year. Treat water in the radiator system every other year with Fernox in the expansion tank which prevents organisms developing. Look for an alternative means of space and water heating (open fire, closed stove, immersion heater).

b. Oil-fired hot-water central heating: get boiler serviced twice a year. Fernox in expansion tank every other year. Aim to get an alternative heat-source that would take over the main load of heating using your oil-fired boiler as a back-up (solid fuel cooker, closed stove or boiler).

c. Solid-fuel (anthracite, coke, etc.) boiler, cooker or closed stove, heating hot water and/or radiators. Service only when necessary, but flues need sweeping once a year. Think of a fall-back alternative in case absence or ill-health makes re-fuelling difficult (immersion heater, portable electric radiant/convector, night-storage radiator).

d. Electric night storage systems, oil-filled radiators, natural convector panels, immersion or instant water-heating. Normally no servicing required. Make sure you have best temperature and time controls so no heat is wasted. Look for alternative heat source (open fire, portable calor gas convector).

Heating systems — how to supplement if they are not adequate

a. Insulation (see above) might well transform it into an adequate system.

SETTING UP HOME

b. Install thermostatic radiator controls so that the heat available can be used where it is most needed, and other rooms kept with just the chill off.

c. Heat hot water separately to reduce the load on the boiler (e.g. an immersion heater is a good idea to have in any case — see above).

d. Get an efficient closed stove in the main living room which will also contribute warmth to the rest of the house.

e. Fit a stove with a back boiler in the living room and use this to heat domestic hot water or to link in with existing boiler to boost its output to both radiators and hot water.

Heating systems — some central heating/hot water systems suitable for small houses and flats

If there is no system in the house or flat you have a number of options and which you decide on will depend how you answer four main questions: What fuels are available? And what storage space have you? Are there any existing fireplaces or flues? Are you at home most of the day or out working; in other words how vital is it to have a fully automatic system?

Here are some suggestions linked to the different main fuels available to you.

Small gas-fired systems — A small wall-hung boiler with either a balanced or conventional flue can provide central heating and hot water for houses with up to four small bedrooms and can be used to provide domestic hot water only in summer. A gas-fire with radiant panel and back boiler is a very flexible answer because the radiant panel can be used independently of boiler and vice versa as well as both on together, and it will provide domestic hot water only in summer. Both these systems can be equally well run on bottled gas.

Solid fuel — Bituminous coal, smokeless fuel, anthracite, wood peat, dry rubbish. Closed stoves and open fires with high-output back-boilers which can be housed in living rooms can run enough radiators for compact four-bedroomed house and supply all domestic hot water. These are available for use with one fuel or multi-fuel. Cooking stoves (single or multi-fuel types) are available with similar outputs. Some even incorporate an oil burner as well which can take over when refuelling is inconvenient or work in tandem with the solid fuel burner.

Oil-fired systems — Although we would not recommend oil as your sole fuel, multi-fuel boilers are available which can take both oil and gas burners or switch to solid fuel. The change-over from fuel to fuel is not complicated and would be useful if the house has to be left in winter, or all the family gets sick and there is simply no one able to do the refuelling. In the country, where gas is not available, use oil as the back-up option, with any of the solid fuels as your main fuel.

Economical electric systems — The new night-storage heaters are much slimmer and more flexible in use than the old monsters. The most efficient and comfortable way to use them is to have them wired up to an external sensor which automatically warns the system and enables it to adjust to outdoor temperature changes ahead of time. (On a cold night the units would take a full charge. On hot nights a lesser one.) This is a good way to get whole house background heat. In an all-electric system top up with radiant/convector fires, oil-filled panel radiators and natural (as opposed to fan-assisted) convector panels. When these are thermostatically controlled you can build them up into a complete central heating system. Alternatively, top up with a solid fuel or wood-burning closed stove.

5 Exploiting the style you've got

The idea of style when applied to one's own home is sometimes a bit alarming. As if one ought to aim for a Louis Quinze interior or something in an 'International' style. Or at least call in David Hicks. While we don't in any way want to denigrate David Hicks, who is a brilliant interior decorator, at this stage it is more helpful to think of what the intrinsic style of your house or flat is, and start from that.

To make the most of any house or flat, it is important that the things you do to it are in harmony with its own style.

Of course people do impose a style on a house which is quite foreign to it. One thinks of those nineteenth-century brownstones in New York which have been given utterly modern interiors — plaster work stripped out, floor levels changed, and so on. Or the antiqued beams (made to look old and ship-wrecked in some garage workshop — 'being distressed' it is called) put in to give a modern building an Elizabethan air. But this sort of thing takes a lot of cash, as well as confidence and conviction. And you are working against what you have got.

If, on the other hand, you work with what you have got you'll find everything is simplified for you. Things fall into place. You can make it as convenient, labour-saving and well-insulated as you like and it won't look anachronistic.

So before you start muttering 'Farmhouse' or 'Primitive' or reading up Mark Girouard about country houses, think hard about what the intrinsic style of your house is.

Four typical English house styles

First-time buyers do not usually have the luxury of a lot of choice. In fact what is on the market usually falls into one of the following four categories, which we will analyse briefly to show you what we mean:

1. The suburban semi

You may be surprised to know that these often under-estimated houses have an honourable pedigree. They were the brave new alternative to the unhealthy Victorian inner-cities, the result of the development of suburban transport and slightly greater prosperity. They answered people's yearning for a life with fresh air, gardens and some private space no matter how small. Their immediate forebears were the rather larger houses built for the Garden Cities — like Letchworth, Welwyn and Hampstead Garden Suburb. There is nothing quite like them anywhere else in the world.

If you think of them in this rather romantic way — like cottages or miniature farmhouses and furnish them accordingly they become interesting and viable. The exteriors can be simplified a little by cosmetic painting but not to the extent of putting plate glass windows and flush doors in place of the casement windows and panelled front doors. Their scale is well

Figure 2. *Suburban Semi-Detached.* The end of the 1914-18 war brought a great longing to move out of the grimy city centres to enjoy something nearer country life in a little house with a garden of its own. So it was to familiar cottage forms that the builders turned to satisfy the market.

suited to the small all-over patterns of Laura Ashley fabrics and wallpapers and the romantic Designer's Guild prints and papers. Some of the thirties Art Deco styles — in the gentler colours and smaller patterns (as produced by Habitat) are also right. Keep furniture in scale with the rooms — not too big, not too grand.

The furniture actually designed in the thirties with these houses in mind by firms like Heals and Bowmans was like a breath of fresh air after the ornate pre-1914 fashions. It was good quality and unpretentious. There was a lot of pale, unvarnished wood (limed oak) rather than elaborate inlays and heavy mouldings. Materials were homespun folkweaves in greeny-browny-oatmealy colours.

The Habitat thirties-looking stuff is in scale, and so are small-scale simple second-hand pieces or real country antiques. But avoid the mini-chandelier, the pseudo-Jacobean side-board just as much as stark chrome and glass. Kitchens probably need a bit of rationalisation to suit family life in the 1980s. Pine units would fit in — so would neat white or soft-coloured ones, but avoid the slick and brash.

One of the thirties habits you do well not to copy is the penchant for highly patterned carpets throughout! A neutral colour through the whole house (whatever kind of flooring) will make it seem more spacious.

2. The post-war modern

These houses are the result of architects trying to 'design' spaces that support a rational way of living. Their ideas have only been fully realised in expensive one-off modern homes. By the time these same ideas have been built into estate houses they have become simplified, less radical, scaled down. The 'Span' house is perhaps the best known archetype and is a miracle of compact planning.

Modern design depends for its effect on very crisp, clean, simple furnishing, and not much of it. It makes the most, where practicable, of natural textures. To get the uncluttered, spacious effect in a scaled-down estate house, it is even more important to be very disciplined about putting in the minimum furniture. You need maximum unobtrusive storage. Luckily the rooms are proportioned so that usually a whole wall of storage — shelving, cupboards or mixed — fits in well.

The style demands strong clean colours and lines. Habitat

Figure 3. *The Post-War Estate House.* Derivatives of the Modern Movement of the twenties, these houses are essentially mass-produced and are often partially pre-fabricated. Windows are large with a strong horizontal emphasis and no glazing bars. Although space is limited, it is usually used efficiently and bathrooms and kitchens are well equipped.

modern furniture will look good. So would High Tech. or one or two good solid antiques, but not reproduction or flimsy stuff. You need to concentrate on plain strong colours or neutrals with good textures for walls, carpets and furnishings. You can go for good modern detailing — like Crayonne handles on doors, and floor-to-ceiling curtains. Or any plain blinds — roller, white Venetian, natural pineoleum. The best of these houses will have compact well-fitted kitchens and bathrooms which look best with storage cupboards rather than open shelving.

And don't forget plants — as many and as burgeoning as you can manage.

3. Late Victorian/the Edwardian

These are the houses and mansion flats built with generous sized rooms, very high ceilings and a lot of ornament including fruity plasterwork and often amazing fireplaces. They are direct descendants of the grand eighteenth and early nineteenth-century town houses — often more ornamented to make up for their lack of size or grounds. Even so the scale is big — very big compared with the scale of the modern terrace house or the semi. You need to think on a large scale if you are going to live in one of these houses — or as more likely — a flat carved out of one. Small furniture, little patterns, small ornaments will all get lost.

Luckily the big Edwardian furniture which these rooms

require is still available reasonably cheaply. So don't build in modern cupboards; buy huge wardrobes. The big formal wallpaper and fabric patterns are still printed. Anything Art Nouveau or William Morris will fit the scale of these rooms. They can take very stylish dramatic ideas, or equally you can cheat very simply. If you can't afford the William Morris treatment, paint the walls up to cornice level in a strong colour and paint panels or stencil patterns on them. Have generous floor-to-ceiling curtains — but use a strong cheap material with handsome borders. These are about the only rooms big enough for four poster beds without looking silly. If you haven't inherited the family Van Dycks, group lots of smaller pictures, or even posters, together to make one unit on the big wall.

You'll find floors and doors, if original, made from high quality timber. So floors can be stripped and sealed inexpensively. Often the shutters round the windows will work — so use them instead of curtains.

Some of the most stylish kitchens and bathrooms are created in houses like this. But mostly it is a battle between lack of floor area and a much too high ceiling. If you don't want to put in a false ceiling (expensive) this is the time to use the strong horizontal emphasis of open shelves set as high as you can conveniently reach, and lose the rest of the wall above and the ceiling by painting them all one dark disappearing colour with lots of sparkling white below.

Figure 4. *Timber-Framed Cottage*. The romantic ideal of life in the country for many town-dwellers. Although in the past they were often damp and dark with perilous stairs, no bath and an earth closet down the garden, today with expert advice they can be made as warm, dry and convenient as a modern house yet still retain their enchantment.

4. Tiny cottage/small terrace house

These are both tiny versions of the Georgian manor house ideal. Although they are small they often have a very pleasant atmosphere because the rooms are well-proportioned in their small-scale way. The pretty original fireplaces often still exist. The woodwork is frequently well-made but modest painted pine with pretty mouldings, which can look good stripped, although the Georgians themselves never exposed wood unless it was a hard one like oak or mahogany. Pine was nearly always painted to simulate something grander.

The colours which suit these houses are the eighteenth century colours — almond green, apricot, sky blue, terracotta, pink, rich beige, with lots of white. You will make the whole place seem larger if you plan the colours to sympathise with each other throughout the house. (The big Georgian houses it is true have Etruscan rooms one colour, salons another colour and so on, but they have the advantage of being large enough to take it.)

Figure 5. *Small Terrace Houses.* Houses like these were built all over the country from the end of the eighteenth century to the end of the nineteenth. Little more than cottages, they were scaled-down versions of the grander terraces and retain the same simple elegance. To preserve their subtle charm and character careful matching of existing features — doors, windows, internal joinery — is essential when replacment becomes necessary.

Fresh country-ish traditional patterns on a small scale will look good (some Laura Ashley, and it's worth looking at the Warner's and Coles' books). Plain or textured floors not patterns — again the wood of the floors often comes up very well when sanded and sealed and will look good with rush and coir matting

SETTING UP HOME

or rugs (Persian, Indian etc.). Plenty of space-doubling framed mirrors. Small furniture and not too much of it, but nothing frail-looking: you need sturdy stuff which looks hand-made and as though it has lasted or will last for generations because it is well-made. This is the sort of place where your own handiwork — patchwork quilts, tapestry cushion covers — will look its best.

Making your own imprint

In suggesting you become sympathetic to the intrinsic style of your home, we are definitely not suggesting you become a slave to it.

It will have the advantage of giving you a discipline within which to make your choices. But within it, your choices will be your own. The colours you like. The furniture you feel comfortable with. The family bits that have come your way. The kitchen fittings you can afford.

Most of us are sub-consciously developing a sense of our personal style all the time. And now, setting up house for the first time, is your chance to experiment and put together what you like how you like it. You are free from the restrictions of home, ready-furnished digs and shared flats.

However, even born designers train their eye and develop their tastes gradually, making mistakes en route. Here are a few suggestions to help you to develop your eye:

1. Always start with things you like and feel comfortable with. This applies to colour (but see below) as well as furniture and finishes.

You may not always be able to afford what you would choose if money were no object. But, as with clothes, there is usually an alternative you do like and can afford. One way is simply to use your ingenuity and discover the much cheaper substitutes which give the same overall impression. Another way is to make-do with something which is obviously not permanent. Like using planks of wood supported by bricks for bookshelves.

A third way is to develop resourcefulness — finding and using cheap objects as raw material and transforming them yourself into ones you like. Sometimes it is pieces like this that become part of the essence of what is your home. Twenty years later you would not dream of getting rid of them if you moved to a much grander house.

2. Learn from other people's experience. Anyone's house is fair game. Your parents' home. Your best friend's. The Duke of

Bedford's. Buckingham Palace. Californian beach houses and Scandinavian forest retreats photographed in *House & Garden*. Rooms in paintings — from Dutch interiors to David Hockneys. Room settings designed for stores like Conran Designs, Heal's or Liberty's. Rooms in showhouses furnished to show off the house. Visiting museums and country houses open to the public is a painless way to become familiar with the styles and colours of particular periods.

There are also a great many beautifully-produced books and magazines. If you can't afford to buy, you can usually borrow them from public libraries. There are the Conran Omnibuses and the series produced by the Design Centre and *House & Garden* magazine. We've found the *Apartment Book* (from New York but available over here) one of the liveliest sources of new ideas.

3. Use ready-made help. When you are on the point of choosing things, two catalogues in particular are worth investing in: the Laura Ashley one because with it you can match colours and fabrics, plain things and patterns right through the house; and the Habitat catalogue because it shows the furniture in superbly designed settings and is full of ideas which are simple to translate into your own home, whether or not you like the furniture.

Then there are the ranges of fabrics, paints and wallpapers designed to be put together. The Sanderson Triad range is one which has been going some time, but is always being added to. Coles, Warners and Osborne & Little have matching papers and fabrics too. Designers Guild fabrics and furnishings are an object lesson in how different patterns can be mixed together.

All these firms have done a lot of the design spadework for you. You just put things together to suit your individual taste.

Putting together colour

Colour is not just a matter of tint — red, blue or green. And its effect is not only changed by light and texture but also by the other colours around it. The science of colour and the whole range of its application is very readably discussed in *Colour* — a coffee-table Mitchell-Beazley omnibus.

Here are ten simple guidelines

1. Think in terms of your whole house or flat. Start your planning around what you have already — e.g. sanded floors, a sofa already upholstered, a bed cover, any pictures, prints or posters, a rug, etc.

Use the interior decorator's technique of building up schemes with samples on a pin-board. Group the samples for each room — together with something to represent the colours and textures of objects. Dispose the rooms round the board so you get an impression of how the colours will react to each other through the whole house. This will help you co-ordinate colours from room to room and build up your individual 'palette'.

2. Aim to have one or two colours running throughout the house. You can do this by relating all your floor colours, keeping all the ceilings white, and painting the woodwork (doors, window frames, skirting and cupboard fronts) the same colour throughout. This kind of consistency will help a small house or flat look larger and will give any house or flat a professional stamp.

3. White is particularly important in this country where the light is often soft and even a bit dull. Because white is the most light-reflective colour, it makes more of what light there is and spreads the light into the corners of the room that are farthest from the windows.

White sets off other colours, which is why it is so useful for window frames, doors, skirtings, cornices, etc. It also highlights textures like wood, stone, bricks, old plaster, T & G boarding etc.

If you have to link a lot of different textures (brick and plaster on the same wall for example) or planes (as in attic rooms or dormers) the easiest way to pull them together is to paint them all white.

White can look fresh and informal — in cottages or on the walls of converted barns. It can look extremely sophisticated — as when floors, walls, ceilings, carpets, everything in fact is white and the only variation is in the different textures and shades of white.

Don't just think in terms of the whitest whites and superwhites. You can get exciting effects with creamy-whites, milky whites and off-whites setting each other off.

4. Convention says yellow brings sunlight into a room and we must admit convention, this time, is right again. Direct sunlight does contain a lot of yellow. But there are yellows and yellows. Predominantly yellow schemes are difficult to get just right, but you will bring sun into your basement with a strong, clear yellow with no green or orange in it. Perhaps in the form of a lino floor or glossy walls.

Yellow ochres look rich with almost any other colour — splendid on walls as a setting for pictures, books and other objects — acting almost as a warm neutral, more interesting than beige.

Smaller areas of sharp yellow can be used as, say, cushions or as an ingredient of a pattern to set off and brighten other colours and schemes.

5. Green is a colour that sub-consciously makes you feel there is more space — perhaps because it links through to the trees, grass and greenery outside.

As in nature all greens tend to mix together and mix easily with other colours. William Morris and the post-war Scandinavians liked their greens with blues. The French use greens with both sharp Indian pinks and soft apple blossom pinks. The recent decorator scheme is vivid emerald with brown and white. Soft sage green with lots of white and sandy beige sets off almost any style of a house.

Lots of greenery and plants bring the outside inside.

6. The earthy colours — the burnt oranges, Indian reds, peat browns, and Thames greens need a lot of white to set them off. As they reflect less light, ceilings in these colours will tend to appear lower. Walls painted in them can give odd-shaped rooms or large rooms without very good proportions a more manageable shape. (But small rooms will look even smaller unless you make the colours more light reflecting by using a gloss paint, glazing over the paint or making it more interesting with a technique like 'dragging'.)

You can lose the bulk of very large pieces of furniture — sofas, club chairs, large tables, grand pianos even — if they and the walls or floor of a room are the same colour.

7. Fondant/ice-cream/sweet pea pastels are definitely coming back (cf. Jilly Cooper says the upper classes are now into ice-blue for walls).

You'll find good examples of these colours in the British Standards range. This is made by all the leading paint manufacturers. Their retail cards include a selection mixed up with what they think will be the most popular shades each year. Each BS colour in the range is coded with a BS number and therefore you should be able to match them up wherever and whenever you buy them. Big builder's merchants normally keep both the full cards and the paints in stock. Other people with

SETTING UP HOME

interesting colour ranges are Coles, John Oliver, Laura Ashley and Habitat.

8. Very often you don't need to have a colour scheme as such. Colour will build up almost without your thinking from your possessions, objects and textures. And you can set them all against a neutral background — beige, cream, fawn non-colours — with interesting textures on the walls and floor.

You then need only small changes in the arrangement of the furniture or the objects, the acquisition of one or two new things and some different splashes of colour, to re-charge the whole look of the room.

9. There has been a growing vogue for patterns and mixing patterns. Things to remember are, first, big rooms will take big patterns but small rooms get dwarfed by them. Small patterns in big rooms won't 'read' as pattern but as texture.

Very few rooms can take two dominant patterns. So if you are having patterned wallpaper, patterned curtains, patterned upholstery, rugs and cushions, you need to work out where your dominant pattern will be and choose the rest to set it off and complement it.

When mixing patterns it is safer to relate the colours but contrast the scale. Or with small-scale patterns relate the scale and colour but vary the design.

10. Another factor in your colour mix is the quality of the light. A south-facing room gets sunlight (with a lot of yellow) so all the colours reflect more warmth — even ice-blue. A room facing north will get no direct sunlight so if it is to look warm and friendly you have to provide the warmth in the colours you use.

Electric tungsten bulbs cast a yellower light than daylight. Coloured lampshades can modify their effect further, and positively deaden some colours.

Fluorescent lights often have a flattening and distorting effect on colours. It is important to get the tubes which as nearly as possible resemble daylight such as the Philips Colour 80. These are used in places like operating theatres and art galleries where true colours are very important.

Style for as little as possible

'*Less is More*', Mies van der Rohe

When you don't have money for exactly what you want, the alternative to compromising and getting it almost right is to spend as little as possible. Here are some cheap (but not nasty) solutions to what can be the big expenses of doing up a place. Look at these ideas in conjunction with Chapter 13 and they'll cost even less.

Floors
1. If boards are in reasonable condition — sand then seal, stain, or paint. Use rugs to get effect and for comfort underfoot. If they are not to look like islands or stepping stones, the background colour of the rug should pick up the colour of the floor.
2. If boards are in terrible condition, tack sheets of hardboard over and treat as a sanded floor with rugs.
3. Some cushion-backed vinyl sheeting almost looks like the materials (brick, cork, wood, tiles) it is emulating. Try to avoid sticking it down, but, where you have to, use double-sided tape.
4. Very inexpensive foam-backed carpeting can also be laid by you. Mostly the colours are frightful, but if you look hard you can find one or two ranges with good colours. Darker mid-tones will be easier to keep looking clean than pastels or very dark colours.
5. Coir matting in warm natural colours is an interesting texture to look at — if hard under bare feet! It is cheap and hard-wearing and therefore a good solution for long halls and stairs as well as living rooms. As it is now available with a latex backing and in widths up to 12ft (4m) it is not difficult to lay yourself. The latex backing also makes it easier to keep clean as dust can be hoovered up instead of collecting on the floor underneath.

Walls
1. If in good condition but ghastly colour or paper, paint over. Remember, silk/gloss paint shows up textures; matt reduces them.
2. Paper over with good quality lining paper (*not* wood chip) in a nice creamy natural colour. Looks good on its own or makes a good base for later painting, wallpapering or friezes or stencils, see below.
3. Use Friezes, now made by many wallpaper manufacturers (Coles do a particularly good book). Cheaper and easier to fix than paper. Use to give expensive effects like wall panelling. Or cornices where none exist between wall and ceiling. Or at picture rail or door height or above skirtings where room is disproportionately high. Or copy John Fowler and use in vertical stripes instead of a patterned wallpaper.

SETTING UP HOME

4. Use stencils. Use like friezes, but you get a more eighteenth-century hand painted look. Buy from better stationers.
5. If walls are in bad condition, the cheaper alternative to re-plastering or yards of lovely T & G boarding is to line with special fabrics like Tasso woven fibreglass which needs painting over. Or strong papers like Anaglypta, linen-woven lining papers or vinyl-coated linen textured papers. All of these have good textures on their own or can be painted over.
6. Granular cork tiles (pale or very dark brown) are light enough to glue to rather groggy walls. Also help to insulate. Can be used as pin-up boards.

Windows
1. Keep in period — both style and ironmongery. Most replacements are available off-the-peg from firms like Magnet, Boulton & Paul or Channel Woodcraft (who make a narrow module range for old houses). Beardmores have moderate-priced ironmongery in iron, brass and aluminium, as well as expensive.
2. Keep window frame and glazing bars white — both inside and outside window.
3. Grand effects can be achieved by using plain wood poles (from John Lewis) and yards and yards of really inexpensive material like sheeting, unbleached calico, curtain lining material. Mount it generously on Rufflette Regis tape. Define at the edges and bottom with a border. Or use Indian bedspreads (from Liberty's or Oxfam) in the same way — they usually have their own borders.
4. Unify odd shaped windows by grouping them behind one floor to ceiling curtain. Mount the track on the ceiling if you need extra height. (Use Swish or Silent Gliss.)
5. If there are radiators under the window, use blinds (roller or venetian) to shut out the night and either curtains just at the sides which you never pull (using less material!) or if you want to pull them, sheers.
6. Roller blinds are cheaper than curtains — they use so much less stuff! Venetian blinds would work out cheaper than frosted glass plus a curtain, or net plus another curtain.
7. Lining curtains is almost as effective insulation as double glazing. Buy lining material with aluminium (Milium) backing. Mount it on Rufflette lining tape and hook it on to the curtain hooks.

Doors
1. Keep in same family with style of other doors and style of house. Match knobs etc. to door style. Inexpensive period look for panelled doors comes from traditional white or black china knobs. Flush doors can take modern aluminium or Crayonne plastic.
2. Break up bulk of cupboards along walls by papering panels of doors to match walls. Use wallpaper of the same background colour as paint on door framing and treat with Gard unless washable. Or replace panels with mirror glass (not tiles).
3. Louvred doors are a traditional form of ventilating rooms and cupboards. They are very useful for airing cupboards, clothes cupboards, kitchens, and cupboards along old walls which may still be a bit damp.
4. Stripped doors can look good even if they turn out to be patchy pine when you've done it all. Do it yourself with patent paint stripper. Be consistent — do at least all the doors on one floor not just one room. If you strip the architraves, do skirtings too.

Lighting
1. Any shades in simple geometric shapes (cylinders, spheres, truncated cones) look good. Shades in cream or white give better light and are kinder to rooms and faces.
2. Cheapest centre light is the Japanese paper sphere — the ones with bamboo frames last longer. Alternative use of the centre rose is to fix three spotlights set as horizontally as possible to bounce light from ceiling and walls at high level, or maybe light a picture or set of shelves.
3. The centre rose can be used to provide light in another part of the room. Lengthen the flex and hook it on to a cup hook screwed into the ceiling above where you want the light fitting to be.
4. Inexpensive track (for a not too heavy fitting) can be made by fitting curtain track (Silent Gliss ceiling track) and using the curtain fitting in the track to attach to the light flex. It can then be moved along the track!
5. Fluorescent tubes give good shadowless, working and display light, but only look good when the tube itself is completely masked by a batten. Philips now do a fluorescent bulb which fits into ordinary light sockets.
6. Reading lights. Try old wood standard lamps going cheap from second-hand shops, with new drum shades.

7. The grandest houses have lamps made out of antique Chinese vases — but almost any well-shaped, pleasant vase can make a lamp with a bayonet fitting inserted in the top. Fill with sand or stones to keep it steady.

8. Always conceal light bulbs so they do not catch the eye. Angle spots carefully. Choose lampshades sufficiently opaque to prevent eye-tiring glare. If you do have little candle lights make sure they are pearl bulbs.

9. Dimmer switches are an inexpensive way to vary lighting in multi-purpose rooms.

Exploiting the space you've got 6

How to make your own plan

A simple plan of your house, garage and, if it is a small one, your garden will help you with every aspect of the work you do on it.

The easiest way to make it to scale is to use squared paper. Think in feet and inches so that as an approximation you can allow one square width for the outside walls 12in (30cm) and half a square width for internal ones 6in (15cm). JL finds that metric adaptations are not so neat.

Shade in solid areas. Leave gaps where there are doors and windows. Put in door swings, fixed light positions (yellow crayon); power points single or double (red); sinks, basins, baths, WCs, etc. (blue); radiators (thin orange line against wall); gas points, cookers and fires (green) and cupboards (double line, not filled in).

From the master plan you will be able to see more easily what needs changing and how — from re-jigging the kitchen or bathroom to furniture layouts or improved central heating installation. Above all you will see how you have to move through passages and rooms and stairs to get to one place or another. This is 'circulation'.

In a little house aim for tight circulation and avoid if possible having to walk through one room to get to another unless the relationship is obvious (kitchen via a separate dining room). You can work out how you will use the house (e.g. how the sitting room sofas and chairs will go round the fire with no cross draughts from doors or disturbance from circulation). You can visualise the way your kitchen will work, whether there is a

SETTING UP HOME

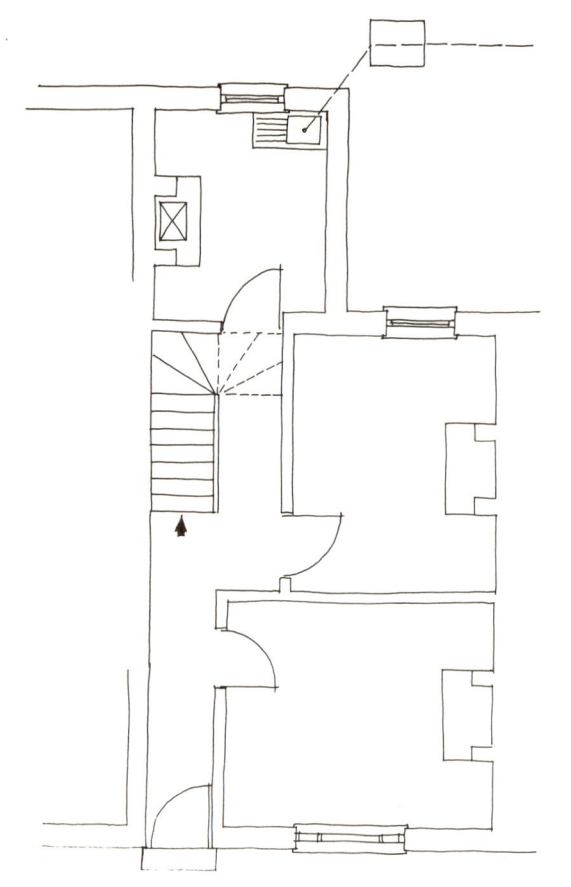

Figure 6. *Before*. The basic plan. How you find the house — in this case a typical terrace house, with two ground-floor rooms and a small back kitchen.

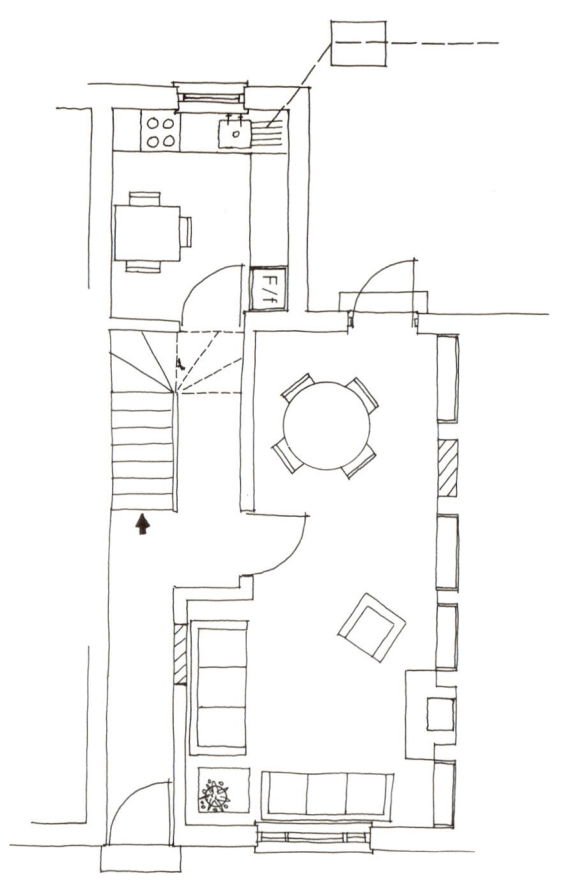

Figure 7. *After*. The simple conversion. The same house — but the two rooms have been opened into one big room. The fireplace has been blocked and the back window converted into a door to the back garden. The kitchen has also been re-organised with the chimney breast removed entirely.

pocket of space near plumbing and drains where you might squeeze in a utility room. By getting familiar with it, the plan will make many problems and their solutions clear.

Exploiting the space without making structural changes

1. Simplifying the whole house with a consistent and light-reflective colour scheme will make it seem more spacious. You will maximise the available light further by hanging curtains clear of the windows, by having large mirrors (or putting up mirror glass strategically) and by creating vistas through the house into the garden with glazed doors.
2. Avoiding physical and visual clutter will not only make the

whole space seem larger, but will also make it safer and easier to clean. Have as few pieces of furniture as possible. Choose storage which is 100% useful (with adjustable shelves and drawers).

3. Make rooms play double roles, e.g. eat in the kitchen. Use the dining room (if you have one) as a study or sewing room (unobtrusive cupboards can conceal fold-up beds, sewing machines, flap down desks and files as well as the best dinner service).

4. Put existing space to best effect without making structural changes. If the ground floor front is dark and pokey, use it for a study/guest room and make a sunnier room upstairs the sitting room. If the bedrooms are all small, use one for sleeping and a second as a dressing room/clothes-storage place.

Structural changes that will cost hundreds not thousands

1. Knocking a small sitting room and small dining room into one (see Figs. 6 & 7). This makes the house seem bigger because you increase the scale of the spaces, get light from both sides of the house and longer vistas through. If you design the opening so it takes folding, sliding doors, you can still have two separate rooms when needed.

The opening will need a steel beam to support the floors above. This has to be checked with the Building Control Officer of your local authority.

If you fit doors try to match the architrave round the opening to those of the other doors in the room. If no doors are fitted line the reveal with a 1" timber lining which projects at least ¾" beyond the plaster on each side wall. This enables the skirting to run into it neatly.

2. Changing top or bottom three stairs from straight steps into winders. This enables you to approach the stairs from the side rather than either end. In the example shown in Fig 8 (in a 17th

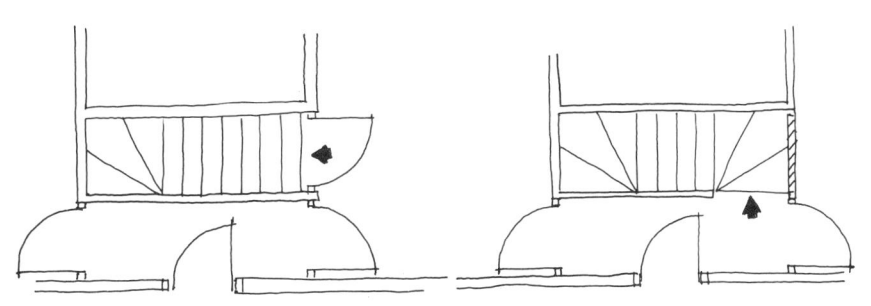

Figure 8. *Adapting Stairs*. Moving or remaking a staircase is expensive, but sometimes twisting or straightening the top or bottom of a flight can improve the layout remarkably. By turning the bottom of this cottage stair there is now no need to go into the kitchen to reach the bedrooms above, as the new winders give direct access from the entrance hall.

century cottage) doing this took circulation from the upper floor out of the dining/kitchen area into the hall.

Make sure the joiner matches the existing stairs in every detail — treads, handrails, balustrades. In fact get this agreed in writing!

3. Minor changes in doors. The swing of doors and circulation through them eats up space which small rooms can ill afford. (This will show on your master plan.)

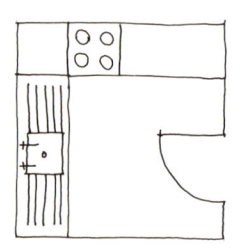

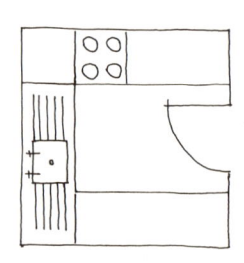

Figure 9. *Moving Doors to Gain Better Layout.*
A   In this tiny kitchen by moving the door 2ft (60cm) along from its original position almost a third more working surface and storage space has been gained.

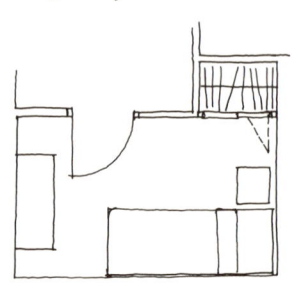

B   By changing the existing 2ft 6in (75cm) door for two narrow sliding-folding ones, room has been made for a bedside table yet the cupboard is still accessible.

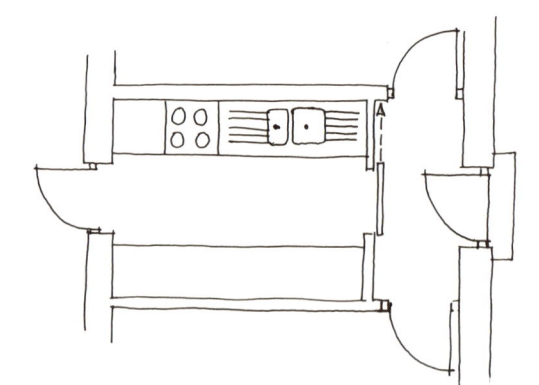

C   The existing door from the hall ate into this small narrow kitchen. An outward-opening one would clash with the front door but a sliding door provides a neat and space-saving answer.

4. How to enlarge windows. Dropping windows down to floor level is comparatively cheap because there is no need to alter the lintel. You just need to have the brickwork cut out below, and replace it with a longer window or glazed door. Match character with other windows in the room. Remember that door frames are

6'9" high so if the top of the window is higher, you should infill with a glass panel over.

Even narrow windows are worth treating in this way because any light entering a room at ground level extends the apparent floor area and bounces light back into the room.

Figure 10. *Windows into Glazed Doors*. Widening windows can be an expensive and disruptive business, an easier way to get more light into a room as well as access to the garden is to drop the cill and replace the window with a glazed door matching period and character in the framing and glazing bars.

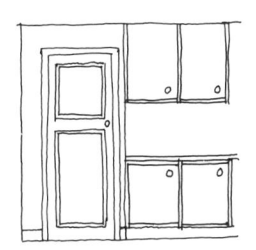

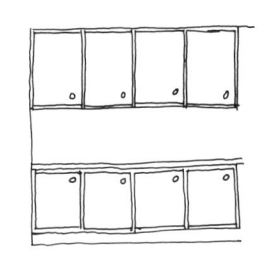

Figure 11. *Larders*. Roomy larders facing north and opening off a cool passage can be invaluable in the country, but opening directly into a small warm suburban or town kitchen much of their use is lost. Removed (they are rarely structural) you will gain extra working surface and far more effective and accessible storage space.

5. Bring the larder into the kitchen. If you have a fridge and cupboards you do not really need a ventilated larder. It can provide you with extra work-surface. If you leave the bottom airbrick in position, you will keep a ventilated store for vegetables under the new work-top.

6. We would advise you to leave one fireplace intact and working in one of your living rooms as it gives flexibility as far as fuel and appliances are concerned and also provides ventilation when all windows are shut in winter. By blocking up fireplaces you gain wall space and some floor space (from the projecting hearth). If you need still more space, it is possible to remove the entire chimney breast — as long as the fire in any room below it is not in use. There will need to be a steel or reinforced concrete beam inserted at ceiling height to carry the load above. It is a job for a reliable builder with perhaps calculations from a structural engineer (who will work by the hour) to satisfy the Building Control Officer at the local authority that the beam is of the correct size.

7. Access to roof space. Essential to check that the roof is doing its job and that snow or rain are not getting in through cracked tiles or slates. Essential too for proper insulation (see page 45) and any treatment of timbers.

Try and make the hatch at the highest point of the roof for easiest access, preferably over a landing where it would be possible to unfold a retractable aluminium ladder.

If there is enough space it is worth putting chipboard over the joists (pack insulation under between the joists) and using the space for storage. It will be comparatively dust-free if you line the underside of the rafters with thick plastic sheeting stapled on.

8. Fit in a utility room. This could take washing machine, etc., and cleaning things out of the kitchen, leaving room perhaps for a dining space. Choose somewhere near drains and plumbing. It could be an alternative way of using larder space. Stack a tumbler dryer over the washing machine or put a drying rack over it. If you have an extra downstairs WC, you could do the same there. If the garage is extra long and attached to the house, you could adapt one end (paint walls, ceiling and seal concrete floor to control dust). Taking the washing out of the kitchen and the bathroom improves them both.

One-room living 7

One-room living, as we see it, is not to be confused with life in the bed-sitter (with its make-shift furnishings) or student accommodation (with its spartan and, if you're lucky, functional minimum). The bed-sitter way of life assumes that a lot of your activities are going to go on outside the bed-sitter itself. For instance, students go out for their tuition, libraries and labs, for much of their social life and for most of their eating and drinking. One-room living, on the other hand, has to provide for the whole range of activities that make up your home-life — just as any home has to. What it does share with bed-sitter life is the delightful convenience of having all your toys (TV, stereo, budgie) to hand to enjoy at all hours of the day and night.

One-room living is an art — especially when there is more than one person involved. It is definitely not for people who want to hang on to things like school games kits, college essays or old clothes. Nor for people who have never come to terms with the concept of putting things away.

Before deciding to embark on life in one room, make sure that one-room living will suit you.

Minimum sizes

One-room apartments, studio flats, pied-à-terres — or whatever they are called — can be any size. Some we have seen are hardly bigger than cupboards. Others, carved out of warehouses, are larger than a normal three-bed flat. The larger they are, the more expensive they tend to be. So you need to work out what the minimum practical size for you would be.

First, think of all the activities, possessions and furniture that your one room will have to accommodate. Measure up where you're living now, where your friends live. Notice what fits in. Notice also how the space fills up when there are more than two people present!

The spaces you require for eating, seating, a double bed, storage of various kinds will tell you how much room to allow for most basic activities. We suggest that the minimum size in practice is 16ft × 12ft (4.8m × 3.6m). Anything smaller requires an almost saintly inactivity not to say tidiness.

There are not very many purpose-built one-room flats in this country — not nearly as many as in the USA where in New York they are commonplace. Purpose-built one-room flats will have one room, a separate bathroom and minimal cooking arrangements either in the room or separate. All but the most expensive will be what is euphemistically termed 'compact'.

You will find better sizes and less boxy shapes in conversions — particularly of big Victorian or Edwardian houses. Even basements of terrace houses become less like troglodyte habitats when the rooms are opened up into one large space. If you are lucky you might find an artist's studio built pre-1914 — which are not only large but also high-ceilinged.

Some alternative plans

Our approach to exploiting the space (page 67) applies to one-room living as much as it does to whole-house living only more so, because you are creating two rooms out of the same space — at its very simplest, a living room for the day and a bedroom for the night. These alternative plans show that there are as many solutions as there are rooms and people.

Making your own plans

What emerges most strongly from these plans is that the size and shape of the room determines how you can exploit it. So the first step is to work out your activities and decide how to fit them into your room on a scale plan — as we describe on page 67.

When you are considering the best lay-out, check whether you have obvious focal points presented by the room itself, i.e. large windows, a sunny aspect, a view, a fireplace surround, a handsome stove, or an existing wall of shelving or cupboards that can be developed as a focus for sitting.

One of the problems of one-room living for two people is the lack of seclusion when one of the two is sick enough to have to be

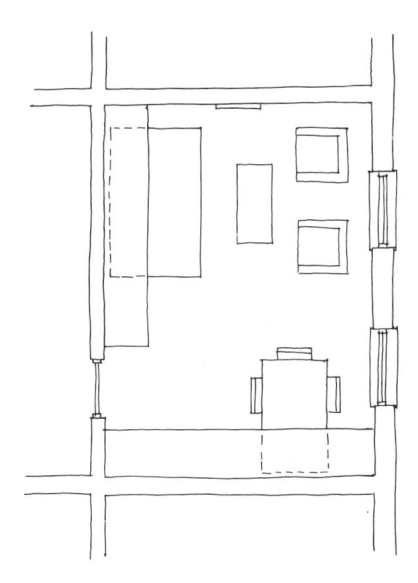

Figure 12. *Scheme A*. This room is 4.9m × 13.5m (16' × 12') which we think is the smallest manageable size for one-room living. Even so the kitchen and bathroom are separate. The bulk of the dual-purpose double bed is minimised by day as it slides in under wall-hung cupboards which form part of the storage unit. Stacked with cushions it makes a comfortable couch. The second set of storage units along the short wall by the door can also store part of the rectangular table — leaving just enough table for two people to eat at. The window nearby provides enough light for the table to be used for work, writing, sewing, etc. Other furniture (e.g. armchairs) has been chosen for its compactness.

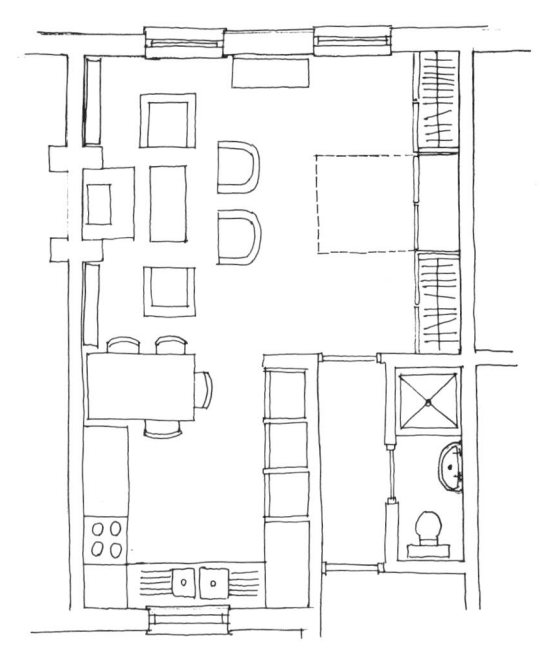

Figure 12. *Scheme B*. This is a treatment for a room of different proportions and size, perhaps a basement flat in a terrace house. The kitchen has been incorporated into the room and here the table is used not only for meals but for food preparation as well as other jobs. Removing the wall between the room and the kitchen does not add to the space available, but it does create a longer vista from the main room and introduces a source of light from another direction which always adds tremendous vitality to any interior. Sliding fold-back doors can screen the kitchen when necessary. The bed swings up during the day into the bank of storage and is concealed.

in bed, or when one of the two has the sort of job which means working at home late into the night. This kind of situation is the reason why some sort of screening for the bed is a good idea. It could be a permanent bank of head-high wall cupboards, or a moveable but substantial folding screen. The latter is a useful prop to have — to screen untidy tables of work or the remains of a meal you haven't cleared away when people, not necessarily friends, arrive unexpectedly.

Try and leave the centre of the room flexible by having easily movable chairs, tables, standard lamps there. Anchor the

SETTING UP HOME

Figure 12. *Scheme C*. This one-room flat was converted from a very large dining room of an Edwardian house in Central London. The butler's pantry and store-room running down one side were made into a compact kitchen and a bathroom. There was only one bay window, so the sleeping area was planned at the darkest end of the room. It is screened from the entrance by Venetian blinds and from the main living area by a bank of head-high clothes cupboards. Back to back with these cupboards, and facing the living area, are more shelves and cupboards for books, drinks, TV, hi-fi equipment, etc., providing the sitting area with an attractive focus. The table is in the bay window — and well lit for everything. The ceiling was painted a shadowy blue to minimise its considerable height and fruity plasterwork.

Figure 12. *Scheme D*. This is a purpose-built studio flat in a modern block. It has windows along one entire wall which open onto a recessed balcony overlooking a communal garden. The bathroom, off the entrance lobby and artificially ventilated, provides space and storage to double as a dressing room. The kitchen opens on to the general space, but the working area is screened from it by a bank of cupboards for china, glass, etc., and the table is close by. Main storage units run along the entire back wall and incorporate clothes cupboards, drawers, shelves, bookcases and a flap-down desk. The sitting area is at the balcony end and because of the large scale of the room, the ceiling is 12ft (3.7m) high, the double bed, piled high with cushions, is successfully absorbed. More low storage allows for bedhead lights as well as TV, hi-fi, bedside reading etc.

visually and physically bulky pieces against a wall. Tables for working or eating are nicer to work, or eat, at when placed near a window.

How can you plan the room with its furnishings before you know which furnishings you will choose or could afford? Architects do these two things simultaneously, their experience of one modifying their ideas about the other and vice versa. We hope that, having read through this chapter, you will be able to plan your layout with some of the alternatives available in your mind.

Certainly even at this stage you must also keep your budget in mind. We will discuss some of the ideal solutions — however expensive — as well as ways to make-do with the absolute basics on a tight budget.

Choosing the built-in (and expensive) solution has one advantage. You may be able to present it to your mortgagor as a structural improvement. In which case the cost would count as part of the mortgage — with all the advantages that it gives. Even though you would not be able to take it all with you when you went, it could be a good investment because high quality built-in furniture and fittings increase the value of the property.

But if you can't find that sort of money to invest — or can't afford the extra on the mortgage — it is much more sensible to consider less permanent schemes. To make do and to spend any money on fittings and furnishings which you can take with you and value wherever you live.

To divide up the space or not?
One of our plans (Scheme C) shows a room divided quite rigidly. How good an idea is this? We feel it is only feasible for very big rooms or if you have decided on the expensive solution of custom-built dividing walls of storage.

Divisions need not be permanent — or built in. You can make excellent divisions with bits of furniture such as low cupboards, bookcases or drawer units — as well as those pieces of furniture actually called room dividers. If you do divide up space like this, keep in mind the secret of good garden design: glimpses down vistas, never the whole garden revealed at once.

Divisions need not even be so formal as that. An arrangement of the seating or the table to eat at can dictate the use of one area of the room. You might indicate it by a change of flooring.

SETTING UP HOME

Fitting in the kitchen, when there isn't a separate room, is best done by putting it into a recess with sliding or folding louvred doors to screen it off. (These doors will provide some ventilation, ideally of course you fit an extractor fan.) Place your main table near the kitchen recess so you can use it for cooking and preparation when you're inspired to make a proper meal that needs more than the minimal work surface.

If you have a separate kitchen, try and make room for eating there — even if you can only manage a deep shelf with knee space under. It will take the pressure off the main room. Similarly try and make the bathroom into a dressing room. Quite shallow cupboards are sufficient to store cosmetics and medicines and they can be fitted under the basin (if there is no vanitory unit) suspended over the WC or even on the back of the door.

Ventilation can sometimes be a problem, particularly if the windows are small and you cook in the kitchen recess. One way to encourage air-flow, apart from an extractor fan in the recess, is not to take screening cupboards or panels right up to the ceiling. Use head-high units or even Venetian blinds. This will also make the space less visually claustrophobic.

Lighting is very flexible because it can change the character of a room at the touch of a switch. Dimmers, spots, working lights and reading lights all have their place in one-room living. Plan for the right lighting for each separate activity or mood and incorporate them all.

If the room is not large, it will pay you to think of ways to make it seem larger. One is to keep the basic decoration and colour scheme very simple, preferably neutral (see page 62). Your one room will contain so many possessions that, however severely you prune and tidy, these will give it more than enough life and interest. Another way to make a room seem larger is to use mirrors. Remember that walls of mirror create a much better illusion of size than framed mirrors.

The basic essentials

Three avenues are well worth exploring when you are thinking about fitting up and furnishing a one-room home. One is the dual-purpose approach: you never buy anything that doesn't have at least two functions. Another is to make sure there is adequate storage for everything. A third is to try, where possible, to miniaturise.

1. The dual-purpose approach

The point about this approach is that everything is much more flexible and useful if it can perform two or three functions — from the bed which doubles as a sofa to the cooking pots which can be used to serve and store food as well as cook it.

The bed — do you use it by day or lose it? The divan principle. This is the old bed-sit solution: single bed covered with nice rug (or Welsh blanket), lots of cushions, etc., to sprawl on by day — a bed at night. Two divans can be treated like sofas along a wall or around a corner. Nothing new and no problems unless you are allergic to making up the divan each morning and evening.

In a big enough room the divan principle can be extended to a double bed. If you do this you cannot be too generous with the cushions. You need a great many.

Bed manufacturers advise you to buy specially made mattresses if you are going to use any bed as a divan. They have strengthened sides and, naturally, cost more. We wonder if it is worth paying extra — unless you want the bed to last in good condition for a very long time.

Losing some of the bed in the storage. If the room is not big enough to take a double bed in its stride, the bulkiness can be minimised by fitting it into a dual-purpose storage system.

A more elaborate way of losing the bed (double or single) is to have one that folds up into the storage system. This kind of foldaway bed has improved since the days when one was an essential part of every Laurel and Hardy bedroom scene. To look

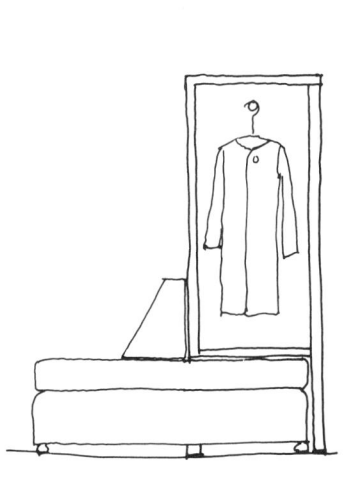

Figure 13. *Sliding a bed under wall storage or a free-standing unit.* A suspended 600mm deep wall cupboard can accommodate below enough of the width of a double bed for the remainder to be used (with the help of cushions) as a sofa during the day. Alternatively a free-standing space-divider storage unit carried on framing at each end could do the job.

SETTING UP HOME

Figure 14. *Pull-Down Beds.* Beds, especially double ones, are bulky objects both visually and physically. Fold-up beds in one-room flats and guest rooms that double as studies can be lost to view during the day to emerge made-up and ready to sleep in at night.

good this type of bed should fold behind doors which are part of a run of units: those tables or curtained alcoves which hopefully conceal the folding bed are totally unconvincing and never look good. To be comfortable, the bed must have the kind of mattress and base you like. To be really convenient, the bed must fold away with all the bedclothes strapped on, so it comes out at night ready-made.

There are two kinds worth investigating. The Interlübke system is very high quality — expensive, but well worth looking at just for ideas and to see what can be done. Their beds fold in all sorts of ways, including up behind a stack of book-cases which revolve when you need the bed. At the other end of the scale are workmanlike foldaways produced by people like Wentell or Rest-Rite. Although these can be bought with their own disguises, it is better to incorporate them into your own storage system. The Wentell double bed, for instance, will fold up vertically so it can be fitted into a cupboard or recess as shallow as 1ft 4in (40cm).

The dual-purpose sofa. This is such an obvious solution that there are now a lot of different ones on the market — from leather button-back Chesterfields which conceal very comfortable fully-sprung mattresses, to those settees made from slabs of foam which you unfold into a double bed. For one-room living it is important to choose the convertible which is not only

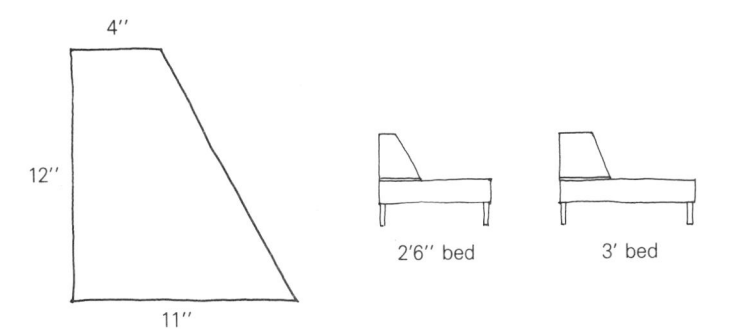

ONE-ROOM LIVING

Figure 15. *A simple and inexpensive back rest that turns a single divan into a sofa.* Plastic and Latex foam suppliers will cut these shapes for you. They are easy enough to cover — simply pin cloth in position, stabbing through into the foam; then oversew where the fabric overlaps, keeping the seam at the bottom back where it won't show.

comfortable to sleep on but the one which looks really good as a sofa in the room by day because it will be such a focal point of the room. It is worth investing in because wherever else you live, you can always find use for a good sofa and even if you don't need it as a bed for yourselves, it can be very useful for guests. The only real disadvantage a convertible has is that it has to be made up each evening and stored away each morning, but even this chore can be minimised if you take to a duvet instead of sheets and blankets.

The dual-purpose platform or gallery. Finally, if your room is over-high you have the option of losing the bed on a platform which can either be designed using space on top of cupboards or as a gallery over a cosy space — for eating, working, sitting or cooking. A gallery always adds interest to the living space as well as creating more of it. A gallery is best planned against the back wall of the room furthest from the window. This will make its bulk seem less overwhelming and mean it does not take the light from the rest of the room.

There are no storage systems you can buy ready-to-use in this way for double-beds. Most are purpose built, usually of wood. In the High-Tech world steel or aluminium scaffolding is favoured. We have seen pictures of galleries made from the pre-fabricated mezzanines made to go with shelving systems in warehouses. One system worth exploring is Dexion.

It is possible to assemble a structure from cupboards or shelves, but these would need to be strong enough to hold up under the weight of the bed and people. And if you wanted a space underneath you would have to find some way of supporting the span of at least 6ft 6in (6.75m). So you would end up with a wood or metal structure to support the platform itself as well as the cupboard and shelves. You would also need some kind of safety rail.

Once you have a safe secure platform, the bed can be any kind you like. Once again bed-making is simplified if you use a duvet.

The table as a desk as well as for dining. It is difficult to imagine getting by without a working table. The minimum useful size with room for one person each side to sit comfortably is 4ft square (1.22m square). Obviously a table which can be extended is valuable. Round ones are less visually space-taking and can fit more people round.

A tough top surface is also an advantage — so the table can be used for messier activities like dressmaking, Christmas cards or food preparation. Sensible surfaces, like wood sealed with polyurethane seals, plastic laminate (Formica for instance) or ceramic tiles are advisable.

There are two new materials which, though expensive, are if anything better-looking and virtually indestructible. One is Corian which is a filled polymer and looks like marble. The other is butcher-block maple which has a natural honey-coloured surface. Both these materials are so rigid that they can be put straight on to a base without the necessity of mounting them first on blockboard to make a table top or work surface.

An alternative to the free-standing table is the flap-down table-top which is often an option with shelving systems.

The coffee table that takes more than coffee table books. Who could live these days without a coffee table if only for all the books you mean to read? Some coffee tables more than earn their keep by being storage units. There is actually one designed to slide open and reveal your store of drink. Less elaborate ideas are to use low chests of drawers, or units of small storage systems like Palaset. You can either put things straight on these as they are or make them more table-like with a ¼in (6mm) sheet of plate glass on top first.

The alternative chair. Two approaches to choosing upright chairs: either get chairs that are comfortable enough to sit in after, as well as during, a meal at the table, or get chairs that are stackable and store away easily.

For the first kind, a comparatively inexpensive but elegant idea is to choose chairs in cane, willow or rattan which, with enough cushions, are comfortable, look good and are light and easy to move around. (At another stage in your life they will be fine on a balcony or patio.)

There is always quite a choice of folding chairs in the Habitat catalogue. They come in metal, wood or plastic and various colours. (These can also have a second life outdoors.)

The Plia folding chair which is made with the seat and back in smokey almost transparent plastic gives the illusion of being less bulky than the others. Of course you will need somewhere to stack or fold them (and their cushions) away when not in use. They can look good hung on the wall — *objets menagéres* as it were!

Dual-purpose in the kitchen. Storage for cooking and eating is bound to be limited — whether the 'kitchen' is part of your one-room or separated from it. The obvious dual-purpose candidates are saucepans which are also nice enough to serve from, and tough enough to go from fridge to oven so you can use them for storage too. The coloured cast-iron ones work well. Ordinary pans are constantly being prettied up — colours, designs, etc. — if you find the cast-iron too heavy for convenience. Good quality ones with vitreous-enamel finish, but without long handles, can be used on top of the stove or in the oven. Good stainless steel pans will do all this and last a life time.

There is a lot of very appetising brown pottery from the Continent which will go into the oven and on to the table — but not on top of the stove, and will certainly crack if put straight from the fridge into a hot oven. French white oven-porcelain soufflé dishes and quiche plates have a lot more uses besides dealing with the soufflé and the quiche: salads, desserts, hot vegetables as well as oven-cooked dishes all serve well in them. (We mention these two types of dish out of hundreds because they are absolutely classic, never lose their usefulness and are always in production so can always be replaced or matched.)

Crockery cannot exactly be dual-purpose, but at least you can start by having the size plates which are not too big for cheese or breakfast, not too small for main courses and so will do for everything. The same goes for mugs and glasses. (Notes on building up sets of china, etc. gradually are on page 104.)

Gadgets, by their very nature, have specific functions. One valuable speciality to have if cooking facilities are limited to hob and grill, is an electric casserole. There are slow-cooking varieties, like the Tower Slo-cook, or ones which will roast and fry as well, like the Sunbeam Supreme Multi cooker. If you like lots of salads and vegetables, a food processor, like the Magimix, is a great time-saver and probably the best new gadget that has emerged in the past ten years. But for one-room living the rule must be only gadgets that are essential to your way of life.

2. The essentials of storage

Working out the storage is a lot easier if you have managed to pare down possessions and paraphernalia to the minimum.

The best way to think about storage is as a whole. In other words instead of chests of drawers, cupboards and bookshelves, think of the way to get it all (or most of it) into one set of units. The ideal is a run of well-fitted cupboards along one wall which combine drawers, hanging space, bedclothes storage, flap-down desk, etc., as well as shelves for books and decorative arrangements.

Whether you can afford them or not, look at the most expensive systems because they can give you a lot of good ideas you can adapt to your own resources.

The curtain-it-off solution. This is the cheapest and simplest way to give yourself unified storage. You curtain off one wall or section of the room; behind this curtain you 'store' everything — how methodically depends on how methodical a person you are.

If you fix the curtain track to the ceiling, this will avoid the problem of propping up a wooden shelf to put the curtain track on all the way along the wall. (This seldom looks neat and tempts you to store too much on top so the propping becomes even more of a problem.) Silent Gliss makes a versatile track; you will have to attach a wood batten to the ceiling to fix it to. Behind the curtain you conceal chests of drawers, a clothes rail or shop clothes rack, stacks of suitcases, card-board boxes, filing cabinets, etc., always providing nothing bulges out through the front of the curtain.

There are alternatives to curtains which achieve the same thing — you could use folding screens, for instance. This is much favoured by High Tech disciples who use hospital screens with the material replaced by rigid panels.

D-I-Y cupboard fronts. More impressive, but more expensive than all but the most expensive curtain, is to use some kind of solid door front. For instance, if you can fix sliding door gear to the ceiling, the doors can be made from any rigid material such as block-board, chipboard, flaxboard or louvred panels. You can organise the panels so they slide open and overlap each other or open and shut into a concertina fold. You can buy a whole system (like the Acme one which comes with a choice of wood panels or even panels in mirror glass) or the gear and panels separately at places like Magnet.

Actual cupboard fronts (Magnet and Boulton & Paul) need more skilled building-in because the frame has to be attached to the floor, the ceiling and the side walls. The storage inside has to be positioned so it coincides with where the doors open. Fitted intelligently, this storage can give an expensive-looking result quite cheaply.

Self-assembly systems. There is quite a wide range of these. Your problem is to choose which one will be best for all your purposes. Manufacturers tend to think in terms of bedroom, kitchen and living room and their ranges do not always combine the needs of all three — which is what you need. One of the less expensive and most adaptable is the Lundia system. The basic Lundia has firm wood side supports in solid pine: pine shelves, drawer units, cupboard fronts and flap-down table-tops. It is cheaper when supplied unfinished which means you do your own sanding and sealing or staining and painting. It has two great advantages — it looks right in almost any setting and it counts as a fitting you can remove when you move house. More expensive, but well-finished is a system produced by one of the Dexion companies — Apton's IP 120 range.

The Open-Storage Philosophy. Adherents to this philosophy hold that you need only shelves and wall space. That more or less everything which is useful will look fine either on a shelf or hung on the wall. It's behind the idea of treating your chairs as *objets menagères* by hanging them, instead of pictures, on the wall. It's particularly tempting for kitchens — all those saucepans and ladles hanging from pegboards or butcher's hooks — you can see where everything is. The only snag, if you do like the idea, is that over a period of years (weeks if you fry a lot) everything gets rather dirty and greasy.

Books, of course, do furnish a room but it is harder to enjoy clothes on open storage — unless they are particularly nice ones. Clothes do get dirtier than if they are stored in a cupboard, particularly in one room where eating and possibly smoking goes on all around.

There are many shelving systems available — based on simple uprights that are fixed to the wall and brackets to which

SETTING UP HOME

you fix the shelves. Spur and Tebrax are two of the neatest and least expensive.

3. Things which fit in small spaces

There is a limit to the things which can get smaller. Beds have to be as large as people, tables and chairs also relate to our particular size. Many of our possessions, however, are benefiting from the current ability to miniaturise — for instance TV sets no longer need be the vast monsters squatting morosely in the focal point of the room. Small sets can either pivot around on a Pivotelli or just be moved to where most convenient. Hi-fi/stereo is getting more manageable — the component parts are becoming more compact and designed to stack; the speakers a little smaller. All this is obviously an advantage for life in one room.

The micro-kitchen. This is an area which can be compressed, if you can also compress and discipline what you want to cook. Boats and caravans have long had neat little sinks, compact cookers, tiny refrigerators and limited but, for its purposes adequate storage.

If your cooking arrangements have to fit into your one room, the most usual solution (unless you want to make a feature of them) is to put them behind doors as if in a cupboard. You will need electric ventilation. The shortest useful width for sink, drainer and hob is reckoned to be 4ft (120cm). Around and under this fit your cupboards, shelves, fridge, etc.

AEG makes a whole kitchen unit (incorporating two electric rings, a sink, a fridge and a cupboard) which is a good buy when you cost out buying the separate components. New World makes what they call an Omni Mini-Kitchen (sink, work top, storage and fridge, but no cooker or rings). It takes up a space only 4ft (120cm) wide, 2ft (600mm) deep and 3ft (908mm) high. Sissons, Pland and Leisure as well as several continental firms like Franke make ranges of very compactly-designed sinks, with or without worktops, some with fitted tops to convert them into a drainer or worktop as necessary.

A waste disposer is very valuable for the one-room life — as it disposes of some of the rubbish problems. But you have to allow for a separate sink for it because if it goes wrong (and waste disposers often do) you find yourself without a sink at all if it's in your only sink.

There is a tiny refrigerator made by Tricity: it is a table-top model and gives you 2cu. ft. space inside. Our advice, however, is to try and fit in something which will store most of your food — because if you don't have a kitchen you won't have room for a larder either.

Hob tops on their own are an obvious way of cutting down cooker space. Scholtes and Westinghouse have two-ring gas or electric hobs. Do you really need an oven below when the slow-cook electric casserole, a portable microwave oven or a spit/grill could do most of the oven-cooking?

Kitchen equipment and crockery can be stored in the minimum space if you choose stackable stuff where possible. Flat all-purpose lids for saucepans and frying pans are better than bulky lids which fit only one pan. The Poggenpohl units (even if you don't get them) can give you a lot of ideas for kitchen storage to copy.

If space runs to it there are an increasing number of compact dishwashers and washing machines — even a tumbler dryer. Try and fit laundry machines into the bathroom. If you have very limited space and money and no laundrette nearby, your best investment is probably a spin dryer.

Conclusions

There are many problems quite specific to one-room living and there are many ways of solving them. When you're setting up house for the first time, you need to balance both the short-term solution and the long-term one. The short-term one is dictated by money available and the particular exigencies of your one room; the long-term one by what you want to be the core of your home throughout your life. We have tried to show what things could form part of this core — bed/mattress, convertible sofa, chairs, tables, storage systems which you can take away and adapt and of course, all the saucepans, crockery, etc. Equally all those things which you add to make it your home — rugs, pictures, books, hi-fi, bits and pieces you like. Core things are not necessarily expensive but they are what you feel you can live with and represent 'home'.

These distinctions are valid whether you opt for the disciplines of one-room living or move into a spacious house. Before you load yourselves up with unnecessary possessions, see how little you really need — and how much simpler life becomes when you minimise them.

But, however successfully you whittle down what you possess and need to have around you, storage of that little is very important. 'A place for everything and everything in its place' is vital for one-room living — especially when more than one person is involved!

Living rooms to live in 8

This is the room to get right first. If the kitchen and bathroom function, the front door locks and the bed is bearable, you can survive. But to live you need a living room. Somewhere to spend pleasant evenings. Listen to music. Watch TV. Have friends round. Express yourself.

From experience we both know that with floorboards up everywhere else, walls half-painted, bare boards on the floors and unconnected radiators lying about — all these things are just about bearable if there is one room which is more or less starting to look the way you'd like it to.

Making it as spacious as possible

As discussed in Chapters 4 and 5 the style and size of your living room will depend on the style and layout of your house or flat. But we think that it is an enormous bonus to have as large a living room as possible. It is not that you need so much room to seat four or six people comfortably, or even to have a table to eat off or work at as well. It is the psychological effect of being in a room which opens out, where your eye can travel through windows to the outside, where there are vistas, rather than walls closing in and shutting you off. So we would always suggest using the best room, the one with the nicest outlook you have for the living room, and the one piece of structural work we would advise people to do on a house with a small living room is to knock through and create a larger one if this is at all possible. (If, as we suggest in Chapter 4, you have sliding folding doors, you can shut off the other half when you do need a second room.)

SETTING UP HOME

Alternative heating

Comfort in a living room starts with heating. When you are sitting, you need an unstuffy atmosphere and a temperature of around 68°F, or 20°C. We have pointed out in Chapter 4 (page 47) the need to think in terms of the whole house for heating. But we can't emphasise enough the need for some alternative way of heating, to deal with emergencies caused by strikes or shortages or breakdowns, not to mention quite unforeseeable price rises.

For this reason it is a great advantage to keep a fire-place if there is one. Leave it in period if possible, modernising the grate or replacing it with a closed stove. There is a good choice of solid-fuel-burning stoves and grates available now: Esse, Logfires, Hunter, Godin, Baxi, Jetmaster and Rayburn all make appliances which can burn anything (wood, coal, coke, even dry rubbish). There are also the Jetmaster Gas Log and Coal fires which look like open fires (and can even be converted to burning the real thing) and give off enough heat to warm a large room. This will be more expensive initially than buying an additional radiator, gas or electric fire, but running it will be cheaper and the effect infinitely more comfortable. As people become more aware of the cost of fuels and the need for alternative ways of heating, quite apart from what it adds to the room visually, some form of solid fuel burning appliance in the living room will be a selling point.

You will have to have a log basket or coal scuttle/hod near the fireplace and somewhere convenient to keep your logs under cover and/or your solid fuel delivered.

If you have central heating but no fireplace, then the small portable electric fire or a flueless bottled gas convector is your most economical alternative. However prefabricated flue and chimney kits are easily fitted.

Comfortable seating

Ideally, in a living room, you need comfortable seating for yourselves, plus the option of seating others more or less comfortably when necessary.

The traditional sofa is an asset. You can sit on it in extreme luxury alone, with your feet up. Or your work or sewing all round you. Or two people will be very comfortable. Three, even on a so-called three-seater, is apt to turn into watching Wimbledon for the one in the middle, but few of the two-seaters seem really adequate for two. If the sofa converts to a bed it is that much more useful. Two matching sofas give any room big enough to take them an expensive comfortable formality.

You get what you pay for with sofas. Down fillings are now very expensive; filament Terylene is almost as good and a lot cheaper. Latex foam is more comfortable and a bit more expensive than plastic foam, but it burns without the lethal fumes. Covers should always be cleanable in some way. Loose covers can be taken off and washed. Many made of leather, Dacron or plastic can be sponged down. Darker colours show the dirt and grubbiness from wear a great deal less than pale ones — dark corduroy being as cheap and hard-wearing as anything. We have noticed, in the invaluable Habitat catalogue (1980/81), the money-saving idea of selling a sofa with a pattern for its loose covers — so you could make them up in your own material, and later change them fairly easily by making up another set.

Alternatives to sofas are offered by some forms of unit-seating which have the advantage of being versatile and also allowing you to build-up units as and when you can afford to. (But look out that they don't go out of production before then.) Cane sofas are a lot cheaper than upholstered ones, but in our experience are only as comfortable as the cushions you provide. And, of course, there is always the one-room-living solution of divan with cushions.

Individual chairs to match sofas — the 'club chairs' with fat armrests and deep cushions — are extremely comfortable, but bulky and expensive. For smaller spaces, the little Victorian and Edwardian chairs with and without arms are ideal, but now just as expensive! Alternatives are cane chairs (but like cane sofas, the right cushions are vital). Scandinavians like chairs with upholstered seats and backs, but wooden arms (which cut space needed and cost). Unit-seating can be arranged as a sofa and/or extra units for spare seating. Lots of designers have produced their 'perfect chair'. There are now several quite inexpensive versions descended from Charles Eames' famous swivel-and-tilt chair. There are copies of bent-wood rockers almost cheaper than second-hand ones but not so beautiful!

Extra chairs can be provided on the one-room living principle of either chairs for the table which can double as chairs for after-dinner (see page 82) or the fold-up solution — like Director's chairs (the fold-up camp chairs used on set by film directors). Then there are always cushions — for those who like them. Big floor cushions are very bulky to 'lose' when you don't need them, so the cushion solution is really rather a permanent

SETTING UP HOME

one, probably best if it is your chosen way of sitting. There are little frames you can get to keep the back cushion steady and supporting you.

When you buy chairs or sofas, it is very important to try them out carefully for comfort in the shop. Individuals vary in what they think is comfortable, but the secret is really the depth of the seating and its tilt — comfortable chairs and sofas tilt you back into them, while at the same time allowing your feet to rest comfortably on the floor. This is why divans are never quite so comfortable as well-designed sofas.

It is not an extravagance to buy good quality seating, if you can afford it, because you can take it on with you when you leave and it will look good and stay comfortable for a very long time.

Focal points

Seating itself does not need a great deal of space. In theory a space 10ft (3m) square is more than adequate for six people to sit in great comfort and watch the fire or TV! Seating is much more effective if it is grouped rather than automatically planted against the walls. But don't make the room impenetrable. If you group the seating round a rug (anything from Aubusson to ethnic) it is immediately 'pulled together'. Plan your group for four to six and expand it outwards to widen the circle when necessary.

You need to think of a focal point. This used to be the open fire and could still be. TV is not entirely satisfactory as a full-time focus because it is a dreadful blank when off. Often a low coffee table can be made into a focal point with low plants, ornaments, etc., all of which is more interesting than a dead TV. Or you can even make a wall of shelving sufficiently interesting — with books, collections, objects, hi-fi and lights, and including TV to be a focus for the group. Where there is a fire, two sofas set at right angles with an easily moved chair make an attractive grouping.

JL's mother used to follow the practice of her generation and have a summer arrangement for the living room which was different from the winter one. (She used to change over the loose covers and curtains too!) You could follow her example and turn the focal point away from the fireplace (unused) to the view (if there is one) for the summer months.

Figure 16. *Seating without a focus.* With nothing to gaze at — gaze at each other across a table of fruit, flowers, books and magazines.

Shelving and tables

As we've said, the coffee table can add greatly to the decorative effect of the seating group, even becoming a focal point, as well

Figure 17. *Storage Wall*. If the room is without a focal point or you are short of space or furniture for storage, using adjustable shelving to house and group television, record player, books, box-files, your proudest possessions and a flap-down desk is a good answer — some systems even incorporate doors and drawer units.

as fulfilling the useful purpose of somewhere to put cups, glasses, ashtrays, even plates and TV suppers.

There is an enormous choice of coffee tables. We feel that anything in a simple shape — square, oblong or round generally looks better than more elaborate ones. And bigger rather than smaller. If you have a particular top you want to use (a piece of marble for instance), you can make a frame and legs for it very easily out of Speedframe (a metal slot-together system made by Dexion).

But one coffee-table is not the only surface you need. We find that shelves behind sofas and tables at the end of sofas very convenient and understand why the Victorians went in for sofa tables. While coffee tables should be about the same height as the seat of the chairs or sofas, tables and shelves behind or by the arms ought to be the same height as the back or arms. But if you have both coffee tables and others, try and keep them in roughly the same style.

Shelving, in the sense of bookcases, etc., rather than single shelves, is a very good way of storing living-room equipment. Books of course. But also the electronics, record players, music centres, speakers, TVs, home computers, etc. If you have some cupboard space underneath, the less attractive things — like sewing baskets, papers, drink, etc. — can be hidden away from

SETTING UP HOME

sight. Books need 9 inch wide (22cm) shelves, records need shelves 15 inches deep (38cm) with 15 inches space between shelves which will also do for most hi-fi equipment.

If you have a very big Edwardian room, you'd probably do best to get big second-hand Edwardian bookshelves. If not, the simplest shelves can be set up using planks supported by bricks. If you do this get creamy-coloured wire-cut regular bricks or blue-black engineering ones.

There are a lot of different shelving systems. Choose ones you can take when you go, i.e. non-fixtures such as Remploy Lundia. Some shelving systems are better value than others, and you need to choose carefully because catalogues showing a system piece by piece can give you a false impression of amazing value. Most will have optional cupboard doors you can add on as well as drawers and flap-down desks and tables.

For recesses, Tebrax or Spur are two shelving systems which take up less room, but only provide shelving. However these two do take different widths of shelves (to accommodate both books and records economically as well as to provide a projecting desktop) which some bracket systems don't.

Pianos

If you have to fit in a piano it is best, if possible, for it to live in a separate section of the room. Grand pianos of standard size take up a space 9ft × 4ft 6in (2.7m × 1.3m) but need three times the space at least to begin to sound right. Uprights are usually around 4ft 6in (1.3m) long, but only need a depth of 3ft (90cm) including the stool. They will take up wallspace preferably an inside wall. All pianos need an even, not too dry atmosphere. With central heating most need humidifiers — but if it is too damp the strings rust! You'll need advice from a specialist shop or good piano tuner.

Eating in the living room

We discussed the difficulties and solutions in One-Room Living (page 82). Obviously a table which can be extended or contracted, worked on as well as eaten off, is an advantage. As are chairs that can be sat on afterwards in comfort and/or chairs that can be stacked or folded away when you don't need them.

If possible site the table where it is convenient to get at from the kitchen and plan some storage near it to take crockery, cutlery, glasses, coffee cups you will use at the table or when people come.

LIVING ROOMS TO LIVE IN

As you use your living room in different ways, you need to plan flexible lighting in the style that is sympathetic to your house (see page 65), again bearing much the same things in mind as we suggest for one-room living.

Lighting for living

General lighting is more versatile if you have a dimmer switch — so it can be bright for activities or low for watching TV. It is useful if you can make your central light illuminate the big table (if you have one) or loop it so that it hangs over a corner of your seating — say a table at one end of a sofa.

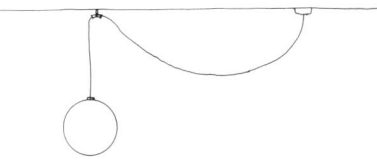

Figure 18. *Adjustable Hanging Lights*.
1. The easiest way to change the position of a hanging light is to change the flex to a long round-sectioned one and using a sturdy brass hook suspend it from the ceiling where it is needed.

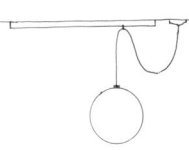

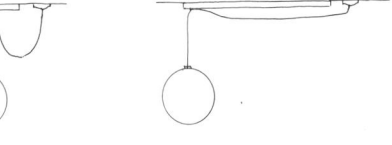

2. If your dining table moves when you are entertaining, a curtain track fixed flush to the ceiling can be used to slide the suspended lamp to its alternative position.

Fluorescent tubes set on top of bookshelves and masked by battens give useful background lighting. You certainly need some working and reading lights. Again the tables or shelves behind or at the end of sofas are the places for these. If you put them on the coffee table, you will tend not to see the person sitting opposite very well, and the flex will get tripped over at regular intervals.

Standard lamps are a good way to get movable reading/working lights and some second-hand ones are still good value.

Shelving is lit most simply by just placing lamps with translucent shades here and there. Spotlights are an alternative if you can keep them from glaring into people's eyes. If the ceiling is not too high you could fix a trio to the centre rose in the ceiling (instead of a general) light lying horizontally so that the light bounces high on the surrounding walls. Or to a track on the ceiling connected to the centre rose.

Our philosophy about floors, as you will have gathered, is to spend as little as possible on anything permanent. But the living

Floors

room floor plays an important part of the room's general effect and comfort, so you may feel it worth while to spend more.

If you have a wood floor in good condition or one that can be sanded and sealed by you, that is the cheapest and, with well-chosen rugs, a most effective flooring.

However, you may have concrete floors or sanding may not be possible. In which case, you may want to consider a carpet, because it does absorb noise, you can sit on it comfortably and it can add a touch of luxury to an economical scheme. If you want a carpet, but not an expensive fitted carpet, go for a foam-backed inexpensive one you can lay yourself. Don't stick it down. Don't expect it to last like Wilton. Do choose it in a mid-to-dark colour so dirt and marks do not show up so clearly. Latex-backed coir matting is also inexpensive, and possible to lay yourself! An alternative to cheap carpet is one of the better foam-backed vinyl sheetings of a cork or timber pattern — which you can also lay yourself (see Chapter 13) — and then put your rugs on.

Starter kitchens 9

Before you start poring over the Poggenpohl catalogue, pricing appliances and planing down old pine, consider what you need in a kitchen. Many things we drool over are very desirable — but not strictly necessary in the starter kitchens of people cooking for themselves. If you pare down to basic necessities of urban living you get to a list like this: cooker, fridge, running hot and cold water, small double sink, 4-foot (1.2m) of work surface, some storage and, if you're lucky, somewhere to sit and snack.

The most luxurious kitchen is only an elaboration of these seven elements. Its efficiency, the way it is to cook in, depends on the relation of these elements one to another — and this is the same whether it is a small kitchen or a large one.

Some basic kitchen plans

Here are three basic plans to show how these elements can be related. And their minimum sizes.

If the kitchen is narrow but at least 6ft (1.8m) wide, you could have a galley arrangement which has two parallel surfaces, in which case the ideal is to have a sink and cooker on the same side. And of course in very large kitchens there are many alternatives which use island units, etc. The straight line, the U and the L-shapes are just three of the most basic. The standard height for work surfaces is 3ft (90cm). (That this is too high for JL, rather too low for SK, somehow proves 3ft is a good average!)

Most new houses have kitchens with 7ft 6in (2.25m) to 8ft (2.4m) ceilings and up to this height fill with cupboards or shelving. (Have a stool with steps to help you reach the top shelves.) For higher ceilings leave a gap between top shelf and ceiling which is big enough for large pots and plants.

SETTING UP HOME

When you buy your house or flat, look at the kitchen with these relationships and sizes in mind, and assess what you need to do in the light of this.

You may find that some unattractive kitchens could actually work quite well with a little cosmetic painting, a new cooker or a different sink. But some kitchens have been planned with so little thought, except to make life as difficult as possible for the cook and bottle-washers, that you need to do something quite radical. This chapter is to try and show you what can be done and how to set about getting it right as reasonably as possible.

Assessing the basic necessities

The cooker. A new cooker can be an expensive purchase. If you want to save money, forget about built-in hob and oven combinations. Ignore the possibilities of an Aga (because it also has to be built in and needs a flue-type chimney). Get a standard four-burner gas or electric one and remember you can take a free-standing cooker away when you move. Look in *Which?* to check current models. All gas cookers sold by the Gas Board have to have Gas Council approval and electric ones BEAB (see page 144). You can save more money by getting a second-hand or reconditioned one, but make sure you get its true history (if it's second-hand) or some guarantee (if it's reconditioned).

If the cooker is already in the kitchen but in the wrong place, it is a comparatively cheap job to move the gas or electricity point. (If you change from gas to electricity, have the gas capped so that the next person has a choice of using gas if they want to.)

The fridge. You will probably have to buy your own fridge and we would strongly advise you to get a fridge-freezer with equal amounts of space for each part. That way you will get a medium-size fridge which will take enough perishable goods for two people for a week and enough proper freezer-space for bulk-buying or freezing things yourself. It is possible to pick up quite recent models second-hand. You can re-spray them with car paint. If you don't want a freezer — or haven't room — a small fridge that slides under the work top is the answer (a freezer can slide under too).

Running hot and cold water. All kitchens should have a mains supply of cold water. Most kitchens get their hot water off the system in the rest of the house. If not, one option is a compact instantaneous gas or electric heater. Another is a gas or electric storage heater, both of which can be fed direct from the mains.

A sink. We would always choose a stainless steel double sink. Double because if you don't have a dishwasher (or even a washing machine) you really need it for rinsing (dishes and clothes), even if the second sink is small. In an upstairs flat (as in one-room living) you may also want a waste disposer in the second sink. Stainless steel sounds rather unnecessarily up-market but of the alternatives acrylic gets scratched very easily and the new brightly-coloured enamelled steel ones although very tough are even more expensive than stainless steel. Choose one which is inset into the work surface, drainer and all. You get a much better seal and the whole thing lines up without ledges, rims and gaps. If you just have a sink and no drainer (which looks smart) you find that the work surface gets swamped with water and to combat this you have to put on a plastic drainer (which can never look smart).

The sink is expensive to move if that entails a lot of extra pipework to re-connect it to the water supply and drains. So you need to consider the benefits of re-positioning the sink carefully. Separate from the sink, but inseparable from it, are the taps. Double sinks need mixer taps. Over the years JL has never found one more reliable than the Barking Grohe Biflo. An R nozzle gives you room to fill buckets and such like underneath it. The plain sturdy traditional tap-heads available on these mixers can be turned on and off even if you are wearing soapy rubber gloves two sizes too big — which is more than one can say for some of the new, smarter space-age heads.

The 4ft (1.2m) worktop. The minimum manageable length is 4ft independent of any draining board. You can see from the diagrams (right) how it can be broken up. But it must 'flow'. Sinks and cookers have to be encompassed, joins tight. The 'worktop' tops provided with some fridges and washing machines are no good as part of this working surface because they are little islands. Either bits and things fall down the gap between them and the worktop proper, or they have little rims so that joining them on smoothly is impossible. It is far better to slide these appliances under your worktop.

What should a worktop be made from? Part of it will be draining board. The rest should be as hard-wearing as possible although there is nothing that doesn't mark when you chop on it or, alternatively, blunt your chopping knife. Expensive and

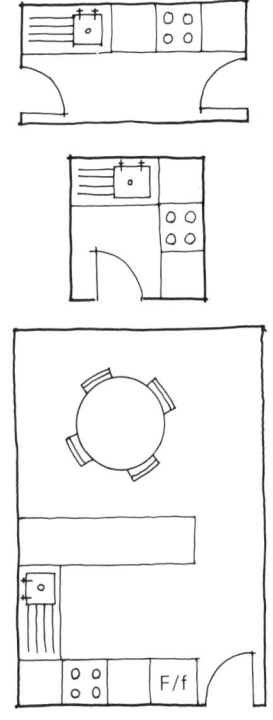

Figure 19. *Kitchens*. A straight line, an 'L' or 'U'-shaped layout. Even in the most basic kitchen, provide some working surface on either side of the cooker in the same work run as the sink for safety as well as convenience. With the last, one side of the 'U' could form a bar unit separating the cooking from the eating area. With a little more space the sequences remain the same but the work surfaces become more generous and full-height units such as built-in ovens and fridge/freezers can be accommodated at either end.

beautiful worktops are made from Corian and maple-block (Woodstock), marble and slate, all of which are rigid and strong enough to be self-supporting over 2-ft spans (60cm). Most other possible surfaces need blockboard for a base.

Eternit is a reasonably-priced slate substitute. It comes in grey black and pale grey. Buy it from a builder's merchant and have it cut to size there. It has some asbestos in it but this is perfectly stable and safe once it has been cut to shape. One advantage of Eternit is that it can take any amount of heat and hard wear without marking. (But it will blunt knives and it bleaches if lemon or orange juice is left on it.)

Quarry tiles (and some other tiles) are another heat-proof solution. If cracks occur water can drip through the joints, so tiles need to be set on blockboard not chipboard for their rigid support. Unless the joints are very close and well-sealed, this work surface can very easily get unhygienic.

Stainless steel is sometimes used. It is expensive. But stainless steel, slate, quarry tiles and Eternit have one big advantage near the cooker because they are heat resistant. To be safe, you need some heat-resistant surface one or other side of the cooker. Some cookers are even made with them (Neff). But you could compromise by keeping one or two tiles or a small piece of slate to one side of the hob.

When there is something to drain wet dishes on (and they need a sloping ridged surface) and something to put hot dishes on, the most economical surface for the rest is a plastic laminate (Formica, Warerite, Melamine, etc.). If this is the surface already in the kitchen, it is a simple D-I-Y job to stick another layer on top in a better colour. It is harder but not impossible to make your own laminated plastic worktops from scratch. However you can now buy ready-mounted worktops by the length from MFI and those builder's merchants who stock cheap ranges of kitchen units.

Splashbacks. These are not strictly part of the work surface but should be related in colour/tone. They are usually behind the sink, drainer and cooker, but look better behind the entire work surface, and usually of some kind of ceramic tile (see Chapter 13 page 135 for D-I-Y). Easier to put up and cheaper to buy would be vinyl floor tiles, or vinyl sheet flooring.

Storage. The grandest kitchen units are really collections of cupboards and drawers. But of course ingeniously designed to fit very specialised needs, with hinges and runners of high quality. The best ideas (like carousels in corner units) trickle down into less expensive makes. But if you are moving on in the not-too-distant future, we would repeat our caveat on fitting up (see One-Room Living, page 77) too expensively. You seldom get your money back. Kitchen units are fixtures — except for free-standing pine cupboards and little sets of drawers.

As most of us have to face re-vamping what we find, it is very cheering to know that old units do come up with a repaint and new handles. Old polyurethane seal can be sanded down and re-applied. Metal cabinets can be re-sprayed with car paint. Even plastic laminates can be lightly sanded and painted with oil paints.

New units from big Woolworths and Magnet Southern stores are the best-looking cheap units we have found. They are well-made for their price. So are units made by serious joinery firms like Boulton & Paul. Although factory-assembled units seem more expensive than the ones you assemble yourself, they may turn out better value in that they are sure to be 'true' and reliably rigid. Knock-down units often need adjusting to make the screw holes the right size and the right angles come to 90°. Save money by putting units only under the continuous work surface. You may find that gives you enough storage.

Cheaper than more cupboard units would be shelves and/or junk shop cupboards. What you need to store we discuss below.

Somewhere to sit and snack. Simplest if there is room for an extra length of worktop with leg room underneath and a couple of stools. Some people find room for a little table and chairs — that's fine. There are a lot of kitchen chores better done sitting down.

If you plan to eat in the kitchen, the room needs to be big enough, and you can find yourself moving into the world of the pine table, pine dresser, chaise longue and plants in the kitchen. Some of the very nicest kitchens are like this, but they are not 'basic'. The simple elements to keep in mind are: enough space for the table and chairs for the number of people you'll want to seat — allow for entertaining as well as yourselves. Enough storage near the table for the things that are used there — not necessarily in kitchen units. Lighting that can cut you off from the kitchen clutter when necessary — a good light over the table for instance. Possibly you need to separate the 'eating area' physically from the 'cooking area' — although the traditional table in the middle of the kitchen, if the room is big enough, works well too.

Making the kitchen work

If you can think through your kitchen in terms of these seven elements, you will be able to glean good ideas from the Poggenpohl catalogue and Heal's exhibitions, without feeling that somehow you're going to need another £100,000 a year to have a kitchen at all. There are one or two other aspects of making a kitchen work for you.

1. Hardwearing, easy to clean floor. The smaller the kitchen the harder the wear on its floor. The simplest way to renovate a bad kitchen floor is to lay insulation backed sheet vinyl over whatever is there (see Chapter 13). You can replace it inexpensively too if it wears out in its turn. The enviable ceramic, vinyl-topped cork, Amtico, quarry tiles and studded Pirelli rubber flooring featured in kitchen books and articles are all long-term and expensive answers.

Vinyl tiles need a more even sub-floor than the sheet. One way of delineating eating space is to change the flooring — but not, please, to carpet or carpet tiles. A rush mat over the vinyl is much more appropriate.

Flooring in a kitchen needs to be washable if you are going to get up all the things which get dropped (or thrown) on it. That is another argument for sheet vinyl.

2. Ventilation. Good ventilation is important to remove dirt and grease from the air as well as cooking smells from the rest of the house. Simplest is to place the cooker by a window, which you open. There are extractor fans which fit on to windows, but fans set in the wall above the cooker are more effective and less visible. If there is an airbrick above the cooker this is the place to put the fan. Up a chimney is no good unless you also put in a special flue lining.

Cooker hoods which are ductless are not as effective as cooker hoods which have their own duct and fan to the outside. If your cooker is not on an outside wall this can be the best solution, but also the biggest investment.

3. Lighting. Fluorescent lighting is shadowless and best for working by. Use the Philips Colour 80 range which gives the light most like daylight and so is more sympathetic to food. It looks much better if you hide the tubes behind a batten attached to the underside of cupboards or shelves over the work-top. In a kitchen in an old house with low ceilings and beams you can sometimes hide the fitting on the far side of a beam.

What ruins the way many kitchens look is a fluorescent strip running down the middle of the ceiling. You need some general light — over where you eat if you eat in the kitchen. Ceiling lights with translucent shades like 'Trimline' which fit flush to the ceiling are a more sympathetic alternative.

4. Windows and outside doors. Both are an asset. If the cooker is near the window have blinds (roller or Venetian) rather than curtains, which could accidentally catch fire. Try and arrange the kitchen so that the working area is not a passageway to a door to the outside. Draughtstrip, especially if the door faces north or east, or it may make the kitchen cold.

What you need to store and how to store it

A lot of things are jostling for space in every kitchen. Food, drink and perishables, pots, pans and crockery, brushes, mops and detergents. They all need different conditions. The only way to keep your storage simple is to keep it to a minimum, and take as much as possible out of the kitchen altogether.

1. Food, drink and perishables. We keep most of our food in the fridge or store it for longer periods in the freezer. Vegetables and fruit keep well in a cool airy place. If you haven't a larder, a cupboard, with an airbrick, on a north or east-facing wall, fitted with wire baskets is ideal. Wine needs to be stored lying on its side to keep the cork in good condition, wine racks take up less space than boxes. The temperature and humidity is only important if you plan to keep it some time. Stores you use daily need to be kept near where you use them (the tea and coffee near the kettle for instance). If you use glass jars, earthenware crocks or pretty tins to keep them in, these can go on the table too. Extra packets of sugar, flour, jams and tins and things not in everyday use need a dry cupboard as they will deteriorate in a damp place and even in a ventilated larder.

2. Pots and pans and cooking things. Try and limit yourself to just those things you actually use for cooking. We find good quality saucepans with heavy bottoms worth buying because they last, and you can use them on gas, electricity or a future Aga.

But the cheap heavy black iron frying pans, if you look after them according to instructions, cook if anything better than non-stick ones. Heavy cast-iron is ideal for casseroles, but ponderous for everyday. Store them where you use them — near the cooker.

A Cordon Bleu cook told us that all the equipment she was allowed when training in Paris was a long sharp knife, a short sharp knife, a palette knife, a tablespoon, a fork and a wooden spoon. Everything else ought to earn its place in your kitchen.

3. Crockery, cutlery and glasses. This needs to go near where you will mostly eat and at the same time be handy for putting away after washing up. It looks nice on shelves, but keeps cleaner in a cupboard.

How much you need depends on how many people you want to feed at a time. If you are starting with a few of everything choose the sort of china and glasses in classic patterns which you will be able to add to when you need more. Some beautiful Victorian patterns are still made today. But equally there is less expensive china which has long runs — see it in the John Lewis china departments or the Habitat catalogue.

An alternative is to decide on particular colours (everything blue, white, or blue and white) or pottery (everything earthy browns and greens and oatmeals).

Unless you are given a canteen of silver, plate or stainless steel, it is also sensible to choose cutlery in sets which you can add to later on. Drawers are definitely the best storage. Or, there are small sets which hang on their own little 'tree' which can live on the table.

4. Brushes, mops and detergents. Cleaning things and soap need to be stored away from food. The everyday lot which you need for washing up and wiping down, etc., is traditionally kept under the sink. The rest can be out of the kitchen elsewhere.

5. Clothes washing and ironing. We have suggested in Exploiting your Space (page 72) that one thing worth doing is to make a utility room for the washing if at all possible. If not, and if there are no laundrettes near, you may find the best idea is to have an automatic washing machine that also tumble dries. This can be plumbed in in the kitchen under a work surface, but doesn't clutter you up with wet clothes. SK has a washing machine in her bathroom and drip-dries over the bath. This at least keeps frying smells away from clean clothes, but turns the bathroom into a slum.

6. As many fires in the home start in the kitchen, a sensible precaution is to invest in a fire-blanket (to smother fat fires) and a small extinguisher (to put out others).

The basic bedroom 10

'The ideal bedroom has a sunny aspect. There is something especially exhilarating about the morning sun.'
THE WOMEN'S BOOK, Ed. Florence B. Jack, 1911

After the complexities of planning a kitchen, planning a bedroom seems simplicity itself. Basically you just need a bed and somewhere to store your clothes. If you plan to use the bedroom as a study or sewing room as well, then planning becomes a little more complicated, as it does if you are having an en suite bathroom or just a basin in an alcove.

The style you decorate and furnish your bedroom in should be in keeping with the style of the rest of the house/flat. As we discussed in Chapter 5, the frilly, flowery romantic bedroom will fit better into a semi or cottage than into a modern house which calls for clean, uncluttered lines and plain colours. Fantasies generally need the rather fantastic proportions of the Edwardian or late Victorian house. While you want the bedroom to look different from the living room, it still ought to 'read-on' with related colours and a not-too-abrupt change of atmosphere. In a small house or flat, for instance, carefully related floor coverings will make it look less poky, because your eye will travel through doorways and get the impression of more space than there is.

Choosing the bed

This is definitely the most important piece of furniture. The first question you must settle is — are you going to try to buy a bed that will last as long as possible? Or are you going to make-do with a bed that costs as little as possible? If you decide on the

SETTING UP HOME

former course, we can only advise you to shop around and even if you do not buy from the experts, like Heal's, at least talk to them about the different kinds of springing and what will best suit you, before you buy from someone else.

If you are going to make-do, decide first whether you are soft-bed or hard-bed people. Soft beds are interior sprung mattresses on sprung bases. Hard beds are on slatted wood bases with mattresses made from latex or even plastic foam. You can make a medium bed with a sprung mattress on a hard base.

The simplest sort of bed seems to be a foam mattress on the floor. But while you sleep it has been estimated that your body loses up to half a pint of liquid in vapour form. This causes condensation in the mattress which therefore needs ventilation above and below if it is not going to become damp and mildewy.

It is possible to buy very reasonable metal-framed sprung bases from people like Rest-Rite Bedding. The double-size ones fold for easy removal. Or you can make a wood base yourself, using 6in × 1in (15cm × 2.5cm) planks internally stiffened at the corners by 2in × 2in (5cm × 5cm) posts, mounting them on Shepheard's castors and fixing battens across the frame to support the mattress. We think the Shepheard's castors (or Domes of Silence) are important for moving the bed easily.

The least expensive mattresses are plastic foam (6in minimum we find) which you can order to size and cover with a ready-made unbleached calico mattress cover. More comfortable but a little more expensive, is latex foam. Most expensive but varying a great deal in price is the interior-sprung mattress.

One factor in the comfort (or not) of beds is their size. 3ft (91cm) is the minimum width for single adults. 4ft 6in (135cm) the minimum for doubles. Ideally the bed should be 6-8in (15.2-20.3cm) longer than the sleeper. So the standard metric length of 6ft 6in (198cm) is on the small side if you are tall. The Imperial Standard is 6ft 2in (188cm).

Bedclothes to suit the bed

Two things have revolutionised bedclothes during the last ten years. One is the Polyester/cotton mixtures for sheets, pillow-slips and duvet covers which are so easy to launder at home and come in a whole range of colours and patterns — it is hard to beat the choice at John Lewis when they are stocked up. If you settle for a larger bed, you will find yourself having to get the more expensive 'King-Size' bedclothes, but with Polyester/cotton you need one change of bedclothes per bed so the difference in price is not too devastating.

The second change is the advent of the duvet. Everyone who has got used to one, wonders how they ever put up with sheets and blankets! The chore of bed-making is reduced to a couple of twitches of the duvet! Get one as large as possible. New duck down is the best compromise between goose down (the most luxurious) and Terylene or Dacron (the least expensive), as it is light enough to wrap itself round you and seems warm in winter, but cool in summer.

If you are getting Terylene or Dacron filled pillows, the good quality ones are worth the extra cost as some of the cheaper ones we've had have gone flat rather quickly.

Bedclothes, duvets, pillows, blankets etc., are all very good value if you can find what you want in sales.

Storage in the bedroom

Clothes storage is probably the most important. But if you have more room in the bedroom for storage than in the other rooms of the house, it is a good place for ironing things, suitcases, sportsgear you only use in season, maybe sewing things and so on, not to mention the clean bedclothes. So, if you want to store your things efficiently, you must first work out what it is you need to store — e.g. how much hanging room and how long? (For suits and trousers you need to allow 3ft (91cm), for coats and dresses

Figure 20. *Well-planned bedroom storage with no wasted space.* This run of cupboards allows plenty of room to hang clothes and all the space above and below the rails is cleverly fitted up with shelving, drawers or shoe racks.

about 4ft (1.2m), for long dresses nearly 6ft (1.8m) depending on your height!, 24in (60cm) is the standard internal width for hanging.) How many drawers? Where will shoes go? What else?

When you have the answers to these questions you are in a position to decide what storage you need.

Built-in storage

Ready-made, fitted-up bedroom storage is tempting — but expensive. Our alternative suggestions for one-room living (page 84) would work just as well in bedrooms. These provide fixed hanging space and drawer systems behind curtains etc. — and there are a number of D-I-Y systems on the market for fitting in drawers and partitions either of whitewood, chipboard or open baskets on runners. Or you can simply hide a metal clothes rack and some ill-assorted chests-of-drawers behind.

Storage units — not built-in

These look built-in but can be moved — either when you want to change the room around, or when you leave the house. For future flexibility try and choose ones which do not look too bedroomy. There is a big choice from the sort of things sold at MFI (which will need painting and finishing) to matching chests-of-drawers, dressing-tables and cupboards from Habitat upwards.

Some units include dressing tables which fit into the run of units and, in small rooms particularly, this saves space and looks better than the conventional separate dressing table. You can also match units to the bedside storage. Cube-kits, for instance, make bedside tables with a drawer and a cupboard to match little three-drawer chests, or double width two-drawer ones. The bedside storage is important and should be big enough to take the bedside lights as well as books, radios, etc.

Freestanding storage

This is a good solution for really big bedrooms because you can still find very well-made wardrobes and chests-of-drawers built on an Edwardian scale which cost less than the equivalent in today's D-I-Y chipboard. But small rooms are dwarfed by these pieces.

In small rooms you really want to keep the amount of free-standing furniture to a minimum.

Smaller chests-of-drawers which are good enough in

themselves to add something to the room are hard to find cheap. When you find anything which could be classified as an antique, you are usually asked a high price; on the other hand it is an investment and its value will increase if you look after it.

Making the bedroom work

Bedroom lighting
General lighting which will enable you to see into cupboards, etc., is necessary. Interior cupboard lights are really only practical with built-in cupboards. If you have a dressing table or have a desk for working at in the room, there will need to be special lighting for these. It could match the bedside lighting which is essential for reading in bed. SK has given up the unequal struggle of finding pretty bedside lights which are adaptable and bright enough and has an Anglepoise. Plain little table lamps with good shades — not too fragile or they'll get broken — would look prettier, but are not so flexible. If the bed is in a recess you can fix adjustable lamps to the wall with on-off switches within reach.

Mirrors
Every bedroom needs a full-length mirror. You can get plain inexpensive ones to mount on the back of cupboard doors. You can panel cupboard doors with mirror glass. These and unit doors faced with it make the room look larger. Only a large room really has space for a free-standing mirror.

You also need a mirror for make-up — over the dressing table or better still with all your make-up in the bathroom if there is room to keep it there.

Floor
We've said above how important it is in small places for the floor to 'read on' from landing, sitting room, stairs, etc. A painted or sealed floor with shaggy rugs can look very elegant. If you really like carpet underfoot, this is one place where you can get away with cheap carpeting in a good colour. You can lay the foam-backed tufted carpets yourself because they come in up to 12-ft (4m) widths. Coir broadloom looks handsome but is hard on bare feet!

Other functions for the bedroom
If you have a bedroom with space for a desk or your sewing

table, or simply to sit in sometimes and watch TV, it is a good idea to use it for these purposes and take pressure off the living room.

Desks and sewing are best arranged in a separate part of the room, rather than mixed in with the clothes and the sleeping. They will each need their own storage, if there is more to store than will fit into the desk or the sewing table themselves. All you need for TV is an aerial point in the room and a plug. Nowhere is more comfortable than the bed with a lot of extra cushions. Put in a chair if there is room or you don't fancy sitting on the bed with your day clothes on.

The en suite bathroom
This is essential for any house or flat which counts itself in the luxury class. The drawback in a small place is that if the only WC is in the en suite, it can lead to difficulties when you have guests to stay. However if there is even a tiny cloakroom with WC and basin elsewhere, that doesn't matter. But if there is only one bathroom in the house/flat there should be access to it from a common lobby as well. The bedroom and the en suite should be decorated and put together as a single entity — carpet running on, colours in the same range, etc.

A good arrangement SK saw in France was a bath with a shower, basin and bidet taking up a slice of the main bedroom, but divided from it by a wall of bookcases up to head height. The WC was outside the room altogether. Even a basin is worth finding space for.

If you have a terraced house and can sacrifice the space, a single floor can provide a very good-sized bedroom leading straight to the bathroom in the room behind. The bathroom is then big enough to accommodate a lot of make-up and dressing table space, and to act as a dressing room.

Beautifying the bathroom 11

When you look in magazines you can get the impression that most bathrooms have jacuzzis, that sunken marble baths are nothing out of the ordinary, that you are living in the Middle Ages if you are not planning to re-furbish with a suite of appliances in Indian Ivory, Terracotta or Avocado. If you are tempted to believe them remind yourself that one household in ten in this country does not have a bathroom to itself at all. Even today. Start counting your blessings in the bathroom in a more mundane way.

For instance, what you actually need in a bathroom is just a WC, a bath and a basin which all work and can be cleaned. The rest is nice but not necessary. If you are buying a post-war house, this is probably all there. But even in pre-war houses or flats, what is needed is often a bit of cosmetic decorating rather than a complete face-lift with new appliances, plumbing etc.

It's important to think what you can do with the existing bathroom because altering the plumbing can be as expensive as putting on an opera — certainly plumbers expect to be paid like opera stars. So we will first discuss what cosmetic changes you might make, then how to renovate what there is and finally how to plan a bathroom which makes least demands on the plumbing!

Some cosmetic changes

These are things you can do if the bath, WC, and basin work OK but you don't like the decor.

Floor
It is not difficult to lay flooring on top of a dry reasonably even base. Inexpensive floors which you can lay yourself include sheet vinyl with an insulating back and tufted carpet with a foam back.

On a boarded floor these really ought to have a sub-floor of waterproof ply. You can lay them direct onto a dry concrete floor. Another approach is to paint what is there a different colour — there are lino paints, paints for concrete, or, if you take up old coverings and find boards, you can sand and then seal or paint them. Very cheap, though temporary, is to use rush matting; it flourishes in damp atmospheres.

Decoration
A good strong colour on the walls and/or ceiling can pull together an odd-shaped bathroom miraculously. A flowery print on a white ground and a lot of white-painted woodwork can make old white fittings and appliances look fresh. You can tame tiles and fittings in colours you don't like by painting the walls a colour which neutralises them. For instance, salmon pink can be tamed by certain shades of bright orange, a sharper pink or brown. Sickly yellows can be quelled by vivid green or orange or greeny-beige. Anaemic blues and greens can be rejuvenated by a bright turquoise or kingfisher blue. Pastel blue by a bright green. Pale greens by more apple green and apple-blossom pink. Tie the colour of the flooring in and the boxing around the bath to the colour scheme you decide on — also the curtains or blinds, and even the towels and flannels.

Wallpaper for bathrooms needs to be vinyl, washable or protected with a coat of Gard. Emulsion paint on walls and ceilings is best matt or eggshell; a glossy finish encourages rivulets of condensation. But keep woodwork glossy for easy cleaning.

Lighting
Lights like the Trimline, which can be set flush against the ceiling or on a wall, are better than dangling centre lights or fluorescent tubes on the ceiling.

If you need a light to make up or shave by, use a fluorescent light by the mirror as they are shadowless. Get the Philips Colour 80 range which gives the best 'natural' light.

Heating
If no heating or heated towel rail, use oil-filled thermostatically-controlled electric radiators. Dimplex make them floorstanding or wall-hung and you can fix a towel rail on the wall above it.

Even set low this type of continuous heating combined with good ventilation will help minimise condensation.

Ventilation

Simplest is to open a window. Warm steamy air rises so it needs to be top opening sash or casement. If replacing the windows, choose a louvre type for best control of all. A glass 'hit and miss' disc in a top pane allows for continuous ventilation without gross loss of heat.

Extractor fans are more expensive. They can be mounted into windows so you use them instead of opening the window, but they do look ugly there, or they can be inserted through an external wall. Fans can be controlled to switch themselves off after a preset period. The fan can have its own duct to the outside — as it needs to with internal cloakrooms and bathrooms. The size of duct needed in an internal bathroom is governed by Building Regulations. Manufacturers (VentAxia, Expelair, Loovent) will tell you how big a one you need, and advise on installation.

New storage

If there is room, kitchen wall cupboards set high, right against the ceiling or above a projecting radiator are useful for storing not only bathroom towels but also cleaning things, etc. bought in bulk. Decorate them to blend in with the walls and colour scheme.

There is usually room over the WC cistern, if it is a low level one, for a set of shallow shelves for pretty things, or a cupboard for less pretty make-up or medicines.

There is room to store the bath and WC cleaning things under the shallow end of the bath. Make access to it by incorporating a door into the bath panel framing.

WC

Renovating existing appliances

Get a new seat to suit new decor. If the cistern is high and ancient, replace it with a slim cistern such as the Fordham Flush. Replacement of WCs themselves is expensive plumbing, even in the same place. Therefore really worth it only when the pan is cracked, chipped or unhygienic. Proprietary WC cleaners will clean up most stains and take off most lime-scale.

Bath

Often a new set of taps, to replace those with blistered chrome and limescale moustaches, will make a big difference to a bath. You could put on a shower combination instead — look at the ones made by Mira, Barking Grohe and Armitage Shanks. You will then also need a shower curtain and rail — a D-I-Y job with supplies from John Lewis.

The bath panel is often very shabby and easily replaced. Use waterproof ply and either paint it (to go with new decor) or paper it (to match). Or cover with vinyl sheeting you have used on the floor. T & G looks good and is easy to make a door in if you are using one end under the bath for storage. Whatever you choose, fix a skirting along its base to match the rest of the room.

Stains on the bath can be metal (from the taps) or lime-scale. Jenolite Limescale remover will remove both — within reason! You can renew enamel to some extent with Renubath.

If you have to replace the bath, when choosing another remember to check both outside and inside measurements, (e.g. a bath might measure a lot overall but if it has wide ledges at the ends and sides it may not be particularly roomy in use).

You have a choice of three materials for baths: acrylic, enamelled steel or cast-iron. Acrylic is cheaper and lighter, but needs careful use and cleaning as it scratches easily and hard water marks it very obviously. Enamelled steel is more expensive but less delicate. Cast-iron (vitreous enamelled) is what the best baths are made from, but it is heavy and expensive. It lasts for years, but you may not be there to enjoy it!

Basin

Taps, again, might be all the renovation a basin requires. Get them so they match the taps on the bath. The plug will be very much less expensive to renew!

The latest treatment for basins is to make them part of what is called a vanitory unit. Some old basins can have a cupboard built under them. For instance, if they are squared off underneath, you can fit a frame tightly under the rim and make a T & G cupboard (to match new T & G panels on bath). If the basin has rounded sculpted front, the answer is to make a low cupboard below, so the basin sits on top. If you run this low cupboard all along the basin wall, contrive to conceal pipes and give yourself a shelf that would relate to the height of the top of the bath.

BEAUTIFYING THE BATHROOM

If you are replacing the basin, think in terms of giving yourself a vanitory unit. Ceramic basins with a rim which fit over the countertop of the vanitory unit give a more waterproof joint and are easier to fit than any other kind. Make sure you get one big enough to do the washing (sweaters or stockings you do by hand) in. Twyford, Doulton and Armitage Shanks all make them. The advantage of vanitory units is that you get a lot of storage underneath the basin in space which would otherwise be wasted, you lose a lot of pipes which collect dust, and you have a good work surface to put your make-up on as well as all the other things you need and like in a bathroom.

Planning a new bathroom

As we have pointed out, plumbing work will cost you as much as all but the most expensive appliances.

Site the bathroom so the waste-pipe connections to existing drains are as direct as possible. Hot and cold supplies are smaller and easier to install, so don't be hamstrung unduly by position of hot and cold water tanks in a small house. The extra cost is worth the long term advantage. The same goes for siting appliances in the bathroom. The great thing is to avoid exposed pipe runs, run as many as you can under the bath or in vanitory cupboard.

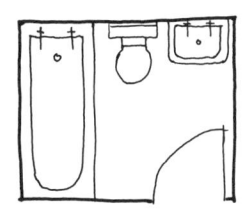

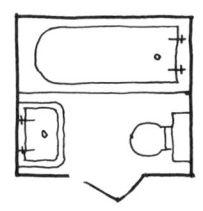

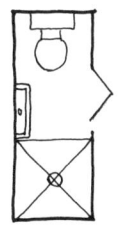

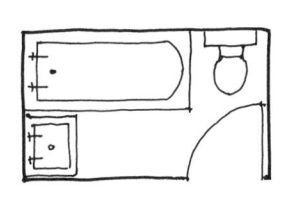

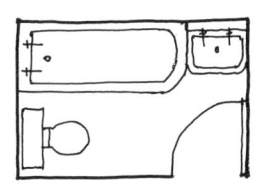

To plan your bathroom, make your squared-up plan and cut out appliances to size. When fitting them together remember to allow for enough room to use them properly — room to dry as you step out of the bath, room to sit on the WC comfortably, etc.

To choose your appliances, give yourself a strict budget, read Which?, visit showrooms and do some research at the Design Centre Index before you allow yourself to become tempted by the latest suites in two-tone Grecian blue. White fittings cost between a third and a quarter less than coloured ones as well as making small bathrooms look less claustrophobic, and there is never any problem over matching a replacement.

Figure 21. *Minimum Bathrooms.* Not only do you need room for the appliances, you need room to use them (e.g. towelling yourself dry after a shower or bath). The examples show common permutations using standard size appliances in minimum spaces.

SETTING UP HOME

Figure 22. *Masking pipes.* Ducts can disguise not only pipes, but lavatory cisterns also, carry a cantilevered basin and provide a useful shelf as well.

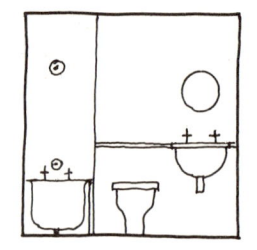

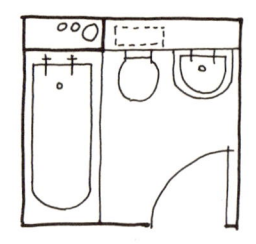

Fitting in some extras

1. An extra shower. The cheapest way to have a shower is to combine it with the bath. Next cheapest is to make your own in a corner of the bathroom. (Or it could be in a cloakroom downstairs or a corner of a bedroom.) Trays are either ceramic or plastic, and come in sizes from 2ft 6in (75cm) square. Get one with a non-slip base. Plumb your tray, shower head and taps in to the corner. Make the two surrounding walls waterproof up to 6ft (1.8m) using ceramic tiles or plastic laminate (Wearite, Formica) or vinyl sheet flooring on the walls and sealing all joints with great care. For the other two sides use a curtain on an L-shaped rail. Properly done this will look as neat and last as long as a pre-fabricated shower cabinet.

The shower head needs to be at least 3ft 3in (100cm) below the bottom of the cold water storage tank if it is going to have sufficient pressure. If you don't have 3ft, you need a booster pump on the shower. Barking Grohe make one as do Mira.

If you are worried about the shower going suddenly cold or hot, get one with a thermostatically-controlled tap. In theory these adjust if the pressure of the water changes.

2. A bidet. You can get bidets with all kinds of complicated sprays, foot pedals, rim-filling and pop-up plugs. These are expensive. If you stick to the kind of bidet which is virtually just a low basin with two taps and an ordinary plug it will cost less than half the price, and the cost of plumbing it in will be halved too.

Get the bidet to match the WC as far as possible. Its taps ought to match those on the basin and bath.

3. Another WC. If the only WC is in the bathroom, especially if that bathroom is linked en suite with the bedroom, you may want to fit another one in somewhere else. Remembering the bulkiness of WC waste pipes, you need to find somewhere not too far from the existing soil vent pipe (the fat one which leads directly to the

drains). The minimum space needed for the most compact arrangement for a WC (2ft or 60cm projection) and a tiny basin (4½in or 114mm projection) to wash hands is 4ft by 2ft 6in (1.2m × 0.75m). Some people find room under the stairs, or take a slice off the hall, or a landing.

If you plan to make any alterations or additions to the plumbing or the drainage, you must inform the Building Control Dept. of your local authority. Simply replacing existing fittings doesn't require permission.

When to contact the Local Authority

12 In-and-out-doors

Whatever the size or shape of your 'outdoors', it will repay you to make as big an effort with it as you do with the inside. One of the first things we suggest is to stop being hidebound about what is indoors and what outdoors. Today you can get the best of both worlds (even in a flat with no outdoors at all) by blurring the distinction. Bring the plants and greenery into the room, and with them the feeling of freshness and greenery. Move, whenever possible, the furniture outside to extend your living area and give yourself more elbow room. As most first homes are apt to be small, it is even more important to make full use of what there is, so this chapter will deal with how to think in these terms, refer you to the most useful sources of information on the plants themselves and finally discuss some aspects of basic care of the outside not covered in Chapter 4.

Creating an 'outdoors' indoors

On the face of it, this is all too simple. Houseplants are on sale everywhere (we have found Marks & Spencer a very good source); they burgeon in shops, offices and indoor reception areas, as well as millions of homes.

Success with your own houseplants really depends on whether you can provide them with the environment they need. Most are tropical plants and the individual species like different kinds of light and need watering and feeding according to their own needs. Some are very exacting if they are to fulfill their potential. Before you carry home the 7ft *Monstera deliciosa* (Swiss cheese plant) or the expensive *Howea belmoreana* (curly palm destined to give a *House & Garden* touch to your living room) make sure you can provide the conditions they need.

Luckily you need no longer rely on the rather cryptic labels usually supplied, because *The Reader's Digest* has produced yet another of its wonderfully comprehensive tomes on the subject with the encouraging title *Success with House Plants*. We couldn't hope, in a few pages, to add anything to this encyclopaedia of wisdom, but from our own experience can offer a few more general ideas which have helped us.

1. A lot of plants need light and the obvious place to put them is on window sills or in front of French windows or sliding doors. But if, when you draw the curtains across at night, you leave your plants between the window and the curtain you not only cut them off from the warmth of the room but you also expose them to cold draughts from the window even if it is shut. If you have double-glazing, the draught/heat loss will be substantially less. You can also mitigate the effect to some extent by having a blind (as well as or instead of curtains) to protect them.

2. A big investment in one really dramatic plant is often very effective. But to protect your investment, you must look after the plant properly. Some of these palms and trees need attention every day as well as careful control of temperature and humidity, even if the attention is only a quick spray of extra moisture over their leaves.

3. A lot of quite easy-to-care-for plants will grow to dramatic sizes if you are patient and look after them. The group of *Cissus* (vines) are not only tolerant but also fast-growing, as are *Hederas* (ivies). The *Monsteras* and *Ficuses* are good if they like their environment. *Dieffenbachias*, which SK has seen looking particularly effective at windows of the canal houses in Amsterdam, need warmth, but will grow over 5ft tall.

4. Groups of plants, even if they are in themselves not very dramatic, can be made to look effective. The secret is to get a good contrast of heights, leaf shapes and colours, etc., using plants which thrive in similar conditions. *The Reader's Digest* book is full of suggestions. We have found the simplest way of achieving a group is to get a large neutral-coloured plastic tray and fill it with small rounded pebbles and sink the plants in their own pots in this and put it on the floor. You can then feed each plant to its own requirements. When you water the tray, the moisture will not only be taken up by the roots through the pots, but also the evaporation from the pebbles will help the humidity. If you have large handsome containers — earthenware, pottery, brass or even old washstand bowls — you can do the same thing by putting a thick layer of gravel at the bottom.

5. Plants in individual containers (especially cane) usually need a saucer under the pot unless you pack the space between the pot and the container with something like peat which you keep moist — but this is impossible with cane unless you first line it with plastic.

6. Some houseplants — e.g. ferns or trailing ivies — look dramatic in hanging baskets. You can use the outdoor kind of basket in wire or plastic or knot up some macramé holders. (The *RD* book has a good section on how to pack hanging baskets.)

7. If you want houseplants to cheer a dark corner, you might succeed in creating enough light by using mirrors. Or you could light the plants — use the fluorescent Philips Color 80 range — for much of the day. (This is how most office plants survive.)

8. Plants which like a high humidity often do well in the steamy conditions of kitchens and bathrooms — e.g. *Saintpaulias* (African violets). But beware of direct sunlight which some plants (including *Saintpaulias*) do not like.

9. When choosing plants which flower, they will look much more effective if the colours of the flowers sympathise with the other colours in the room!

10. In August/September remember to organise some bulbs for indoors. It's much cheaper to grow them yourself than buy them later!

11. More houseplants die from over-watering than under-watering so consult the *RD* book for guidance. There are self-watering pots, but these are an expensive investment.

12. Hydro-culture, pioneered over here by Rochfords, is a way of growing plants in water rather than soil and adding the nutrients they need to the water. It is expensive to set up, with the correct containers and clay pebbles, etc., but works well when you have.

Half-way outdoors — the window box, balcony, hanging basket, etc.

If you have a tiny space — a front step, a porch, a sliver of a balcony too small to fit a chair on — you can grow a great variety of plants which other people grow in their gardens. You will have to choose what you grow both in terms of how they will look from inside and, especially with window boxes, how they will help the outside look of the place.

1. If the plants are in containers (e.g. pots or window-boxes), you can ring the changes through the seasons using bulbs and annuals, replanting every three or four months as they do in the Royal Parks, or you can cultivate small trees and shrubs which will be more or less permanent. Climbers are especially valuable in small spaces as they give you the maximum amount of leaf/flower for the minimum amount of pot or ground space.

2. When choosing your pots or containers try and keep them in the same family — so they go together. Simple shapes always look best and 'natural colours'. When planting them, if you keep to one type and colour of flowering plant per pot, you will get a much more effective display.

3. Providing the container is big enough, you can grow trees and shrubs in containers as well as smaller plants. You will have to give them the sun/shade positions they prefer, and make sure you feed and water them according to their type. A friend of ours who looks after the terraces and patios of the rich makes a weekly visit to check up and waters even if it has been raining because the area of the pot cannot collect enough moisture for its plants whether they are big or small.

4. Window boxes need to be securely placed — either firmly attached to the wall, or else on a strong window sill — because damp soil is heavy. Planting a window box needs the same system as planting a pot or other container — there must be a bottom layer of crocks or shards to help drain away excess moisture.

5. With window boxes, it is particularly important to plan a rotation to keep them looking interesting all year round. You might put in frost-hardy evergreens in winter with an underplanting of bulbs to come up in spring. Then you can change to the summer annuals in May.

6. Hanging baskets need a strong bracket to hang from. You could keep them going with ivies through the winter, but most people only use them for the summer annuals.

7. If you only have room for a few pots on an outside window sill and it is a sunny one, you can grow a wide variety of herbs as they do not like to be too wet, and need a lot of sun. Special parsley pots are good if you can get them going.

8. Other vegetables are harder to grow in confined spaces in quantities that make a meaningful contribution to the larder. However we've seen tomatoes and runner beans growing decoratively and productively from Gro-bags on sunny window sills.

The room outside

If you have enough space outside to sit out on, you have the first necessary ingredient for a 'room outside'. It makes all the difference to life in the summer if you can sit out and enjoy the sun, sunbathe, have meals out, barbecue, etc. and is probably why most people prefer the scope a country or suburban garden gives them to what is available at the same price in the centre of a city. The creation of this room outside has been comprehensively described by John Brookes in his book, *Room Outside*. It is full of ideas and information on everything from how to lay the paving to which plants will grow where. Things you should consider carefully are:

1. Space outdoors is an even bigger asset if you can relate it to space inside satisfactorily, for example, if access to it is easy enough for you to take advantage of all the fleeting moments of sunshine as well as the few hot days of summer. If you want to eat out, a way to and from the kitchen which is direct is a good idea. If there is access from the sitting room you can move chairs in and out easily as well as extending the room visually into the garden.

2. The sitting/eating area really needs to be paved. It is not very difficult to do this yourself. The Cement and Concrete Association has a very good leaflet to help you set about the task and the trusty *Reader's Digest Do-it-Yourself Manual* has detailed instructions.

While York stone is beautiful, there are lots of cheaper, easier-to-handle substitutes, at both builders' merchants and garden centres. When you choose, get paving that is sympathetic to the style of your house. Bradstone's Cotswold Slabs are a sympathetic creamy colour which will look warm and show off any green leaves you grow around it. Stick to natural stoney colours and if they 'read on' from the colour of the living room floor you will have created a greater illusion of extra space. Get non-slip surfaces if possible. Keep crazy paving for cottages and semis.

3. If you want to grow things in the gaps between the paving stones, sow seeds thickly so there is as little room as possible for the weeds. Or leave out a paver and plant in the space. If you don't want things to grow in the gaps, JL has found brushing over a mixture of 1 cement:1 sand is often more successful than the more traditional 1:3 or 1:4 mixture.

4. Some furniture will be able to stay out all the time — and it is good to have one permanent seat in hardwood or cast aluminium. Nearly all other garden seats — loungers, St. Tropez chairs, cane things — cannot be left out in bad summer weather let alone the winter. If you have this sort of furniture, you will need somewhere very convenient to store it. The alternative is to have this kind of furniture in your living room and simply wheel it out when the sun shines!

5. If you grow plants or trees in pots on your terrace all we have said about this in the previous section applies here too. The most successful pots are simple shapes. Keep your pots within the same family if possible i.e. all terracotta.

6. You should also think about screening — from the wind, the neighbours, or even your own dustbins. It isn't difficult to put up a trellis or pergola (John Brookes' book tells you how to do the latter) on which you can grow fast-growing, preferably evergreen climbers up or along, like the evergreen honeysuckle, *Lonicera halliana*, which has the bonus of beautifully-scented flowers. If you need only the screening in summer, you have a wider choice from all the deciduous climbers like vines.

7. If there is room to grow more, but not much more, you need to choose what you grow carefully. Get things which are interesting at different times of the year, not just for a glorious two weeks (shrubs and trees which have blossom and berries, autumn colour and interesting bark for the winter, evergreens which produce sweet-smelling flowers). Remember there are upright (or fastigiate) varieties of most trees. And you can cut back many shrubs to stay the size that you want them to become.

The bigger garden

This is any garden in which there is more space than you need to sit in, stretching from the suburban plot through to stockbroker-size places with lawns, paddocks and even swimming pools. It is really up to you to decide how you want to use it. But whether you grow veg, play tennis or plant a forest in the distant acres, what happens near the house is the same. The sitting-out space, the room outside, has to be related to the house. The planting immediately outside and around the house is something you will notice more than that farther away and so it is the place for special things — pots, urns, etc. John Brookes has produced another book *The Small Garden* which is full of helpful ideas for smaller gardens and a good start for anyone who hasn't thought much about gardens before.

Basic care for the outside fabric

As houses are judged by their outside appearance more often than not this is an important part of keeping up if not increasing the value of yours.

1. Just as we suggest the style of the house itself should influence what you do inside, it should also influence how you treat the outside. A little Georgian terrace house, for example, can take the formal prettiness of window boxes, a semi can have its cottage-ness emphasized with roses and honeysuckle, while a modern estate house needs smooth lawns and groups of trees and shrubs with handsome contrasting leaves.

2. Tackle the outside of the house in the same way. Stick to the original style and features of the house as far as possible and, if there are local traditions, follow them too.

   If the pipes and gutters are few and orderly, they look best painted black or grey — or left black or grey if they are plastic. But if there is a tangle of pipes, camouflage them by matching them to the wall colour (plastic guttering can be painted).

3. Front doors need to lead you to them and indicate the way into the house, which is why they often have porches or canopies and are painted a different colour to look inviting. Choose a colour which looks good with the fabric of the house and the rest of the street. The traditional colours for old houses are soft grey-blues, sage greens, beiges and warm greys. Choose the knobs and knockers in styles that fit the house (not wrought iron for estate modern!).

4. Wood fences look their best in plain wood (treated) or black, white or soft greeny greys. Wrought iron railings are traditionally painted black to set off the delicate lines, but cast iron can look good as well, painted white if the house is a contrasting colour.

5. Lighting outdoors is best kept simple. The Trimline wall light or an outdoor spotlight is usually enough to light the path or the terrace where you sit.

6. Treat the outbuildings — garage, garden shed, coal hole, dustbin screens — with the same discretion, linking them if possible to the house. Or, if they are not good to look at, by disguising them as quickly as possible with climbers and creepers. *Lonicera halliana*, the evergreen honeysuckle, is a good cover. If you want something really fast *Polygonum baldischuanum* (Russian vine) is not called Mile-a-Minute for nothing!

What you can do if you try 13

If you are already a do-it-yourselfer, skip this chapter. You'll have picked up a lot of the suggestions we have made throughout the book and decided which to follow up and which not.

If you have been baffled by some of our D-I-Y ideas, this chapter may get you started off doing some things for yourself.

We have selected ten D-I-Y jobs on the basis of what will save you most money and what we think almost everybody can tackle if they give it a bit of thought and take a little time and trouble. We hope to show you how to start off and what to avoid, what to aim for, so that if you are inexperienced you can take up one of the manuals of detailed instructions, see what they're on about and get going.

Painting the walls and ceilings

There's a strong motivation for you to do your own decorating. If you do it yourself, all it costs you is your time and the price of the materials you use. If someone else does it, you can reckon it will easily cost you ten times as much.

What's more, very often you will do it as well as, if not better than, many professional decorators, simply because you can take more time. There are eight things which help you get a good result.

1. Preparation. Be prepared to spend enough time on preparation. The aim of all preparation is to get a firm, smooth, clean, dry, grease-free surface for the paint to adhere to. That is why, however good the surface seems already, you always need to remove dust from all the cornices, door tops and window frames as well as the wall itself; then wash it all down thoroughly. Use Surf, Tide or similar and a rough plastic sponge.

Rinse with clean water and allow to dry. If you are going to paint over wallpaper use as little water as possible or the wallpaper may start peeling off! Test a corner to see how it reacts first.

2. The first time you paint, choose a wall in good condition. If there are tiny holes and cracks fill them with Polyfilla or Tetrion. Use a ready-mixed product so you get the consistency right and follow instructions carefully. The secret of getting it flush is to wipe it over with a damp cloth just before the Polyfilla has completely dried. Fine sandpaper will also smooth it down — and look after any other small bumps on the wall surface.

3. Choose a good brand of emulsion paint and stick to the one brand. Follow instructions. Emulsion acts as an undercoat and top coat and you can wash out your brushes in washing-up liquid and water. As a first coat on bare plaster it needs diluting with water. Emulsion paint comes in silk, gloss and matt finishes. On new plaster always use one that is permeable.

4. Get good quality brushes (a 4 inch and a 1 inch brush to start with) or rollers. Look after them by washing them properly when you finish each day.

5. Start painting in one corner of the room. Work down in vertical stripes (2—3ft wide) all the way round the room. Do the ceiling in the same way.

6. If the first coat does not cover well, put on a second and if necessary a third.

7. Once you've managed walls in good condition you can tackle rougher walls. They will need more smoothing and filling. But if there are signs of damp (brown stains, crumbly plaster) get this treated first.

8. For techniques and tools, the *Reader's Digest* do-it-yourself manual on decorating is still the most comprehensive guide we've seen. For unusual ideas and finishes, when you've got the hang of things, look at Jocasta Innes' *Paint Magic*.

Wallpapering the walls

When father papered the parlour,
You couldn't see him for paste.
Slapping it here, slapping it there
Paste and paper everywhere.
Ma was stuck to the ceiling,
The kids were stuck to the floor,
You never saw such a family,
So stuck up before!

VICTORIAN SONG

Wallpapering seems complicated until you've tried it — when most people find it's the quickest way to decorate a room.

1. The first time you paper a room, choose a paper with a pattern that is easy to match — e.g. all-over Laura Ashley sprigs or a paper that looks more like a texture/colour than a definite pattern. Make sure it is well trimmed. Get one roll more than you reckon you'll need plus plenty of the manufacturer's recommended adhesive. Bathrooms and kitchens need one that resists steam.

2. Start on as simple and square a wall as possible in a good condition. You can paper over anything that is fairly smooth and clean — but not vinyl coated papers.

3. Preparation — as for painting. Wash down previous paint, dampwipe previous paper with a plastic sponge. Go over a gloss or semi-gloss painted wall with fine sandpaper to give a key, i.e. a rough surface so that the paper can adhere to it. Size, which is just a very dilute form of glue, is necessary to seal and bind new plaster or any absorbent existing paper — you can make a size from Polycell paste following the instructions. Size also prevents the wallpaper paste drying too quickly.

4. Tools. Most can be hired, including a table, ladders, etc. Most helpful is the rubber roller for sealing joints. Essential is a plumb-line for getting the first vertical line true.

5. Plan layout carefully. If there is a focal point to a room start with the paper centred on its centre, e.g. if there is a fireplace, centre the first roll of paper on it, then work on taking the pattern complete round corners — but not paper itself; the walls are never true enough. If papering over existing paper avoid the old and new joints coinciding.

6. Techniques are very well described in the *Reader's Digest* D-I-Y manual on decorating. The crucial thing is to use the plumb-line to get the first piece you hang truly vertical and go on testing.

7. Don't attempt vinyl papers until you have some experience, or ceilings until you have had a lot of experience.

8. Putting up borders or friezes (see Style page 63) is the same as putting up wallpaper. You need to use the plumb-line on each vertical and a spirit-level for each horizontal line.

9. Walls in bad condition can sometimes be rescued (rather than replastered) by papering with textured papers — such as Sanderson's linen weaves, or the more embossed Anaglypta or Lincrusta papers. Tasso woven fibre glass is also put on like a

SETTING UP HOME

paper, but with its own adhesive. If can hold together fragile plaster but needs painting on top.

10. Lining paper is very cheap, so buy the best quality. This is a pleasant natural colour and can be left plain or painted over. As a base to paint over you hang it vertically. To paper over, you run it horizontally round the room.

Decorating the woodwork

Decorating the woodwork — the doors, window frames, skirtings, architraves and so on — is even more labour-intensive than painting walls. So you save that much more by doing it yourself.

1. Preparation. This is what will repay all your time and trouble and why you can do a better job than the professional if you take the time. But start with woodwork in good condition the first time you try.

2. Remove all handles, knobs, plates, letter-boxes, etc.

3. Preparation consists of first getting a clean surface — by washing and rinsing thoroughly; one of those green Scotch pads is useful. Then get a smooth surface by sanding and filling any cracks, holes or flaked paint with the appropriate Polyfilla or wood filler. Finally, you need to sand all the old gloss paint lightly to give the new coat of paint a 'key' to adhere to.

4. New wood, after a special priming coat, is traditionally painted with oil-based gloss or semi-gloss paint over one or two coats of oil-based undercoat. If you are repainting in the same colour, one or two gloss coats might be enough. It is important to stick to the same brand for top coat and undercoat and primer to get the best results and to follow the instructions on the tin carefully. Let each coat dry and sand it smooth before putting on the next coat.

5. Non-drip paints are easiest for beginners, but if you use ordinary oil-based gloss paints, the tip from professionals is: never dip the brush more than one-quarter of an inch (6mm) into the paint and knock rather than scrape the brush gently against the top of the tin to take off any surplus.

6. There are special brushes, called 'cutting-in' tools for doing straight lines and the glazing bars on windows. Masking tape bought from any stationers helps keep paint or gloss off the surrounding wallpaper and simply peels off afterwards.

7. There is a time-honoured system for painting doors and windows. It is described in the *Reader's Digest* manual.

Basically, you start in the middle and work out.

8. If the paint is in very bad condition or you want to strip it to leave the wood plain, it is safer to use a patent paint stripper rather than a blow-lamp for the first time. Wash, sand and fill as above.

9. Unpainted or stripped wood can be sealed with a colourless polyurethane seal (like Ronseal) or tinted first in a wider range of colours with a non-varnish stain (Ronseal, Solignum, Cuprinol, Sikkens are some of the firms making these). These stains are semi-transparent and can make poor quality wood look more interesting. Follow instructions and keep to the same brand for all coats. These preservative stains can be used on un-painted external woodwork as well.

10. Painted external woodwork needs more protection than wood inside the house, therefore more care in the preparation and painting. Full gloss must always be used.

11. Metal windows and radiators are usually painted with gloss paint just like wood. But preparation must first include rust-removal and a coat of correct metal primer.

Floor treatments — sanding then sealing or painting

As covering floors with anything works out expensive, these are ways to make the most of the wood floors you have. Many floors which look depressing can be sanded down and, with a lot of effort, but not much money, made to look very handsome.

1. Pre-sanding preparation, which must be done thoroughly, is to knock down all nails at least ¼ inch (6mm) into the boards and lift out all old tacks. Remove everything from the room so it is completely bare.

2. Old floors especially those with black gunge and polish and stain, will have to be sanded down. Hire a sander — not too big a one — to do the main floor. This will do the middle area but may not get into corners for which you'll need a small sander — usually available from the people you hire the big one from. You would probably find it simpler to sand a new floor, or an old floor you plan to paint, by hand. After sanding you may need to fill in holes, cracks, etc. Use a wood filler which you can match to the wood by staining it with a solution of instant coffee, experiment for strength. Vacuum both the floor and the room thoroughly.

3. Plain sealing with a polyurethane seal needs four coats for pine floors, three for hardwood like oak. Dilute first coat by 20%

SETTING UP HOME

with thinners. Brush on the first coats very thinly and sand lightly between coats. Apply final coat with a cloth.

4. For staining floors use one of the non-varnish wood stains for floors made by Ronseal, Solignum, Cuprinol, Sikkens. Follow instructions.

5. Painting. As you are covering up the wood, you do not need to sand so rigorously, but the surface must be clean and smooth and free from grease and old polish, etc. This is why painting the floor is a good solution for hall and stairs. Use a Polyurethane paint (such as Polybond Q19 or ICI Silthane) following instructions and giving an extra top coat. Sand down between coats. Save a small tin of the colour for re-touching later.

6. There are lots of possibilities for stencilling, painting patterns and even painting on a *trompe l'oeil* carpet using different paints and varnishes, which are beautifully illustrated in Jocasta Innes' *Paint Magic*.

Figure 23. *Laying hardboard panels on boarded floors.* Where there are no projections such as chimney breasts or hearths to negotiate it is generally best to lay panels lengthwise across the width of the room. But with projections it may look less fussy and demand less cutting to run the panels lengthwise down the length of the room.

Floor treatments — laying hardboard

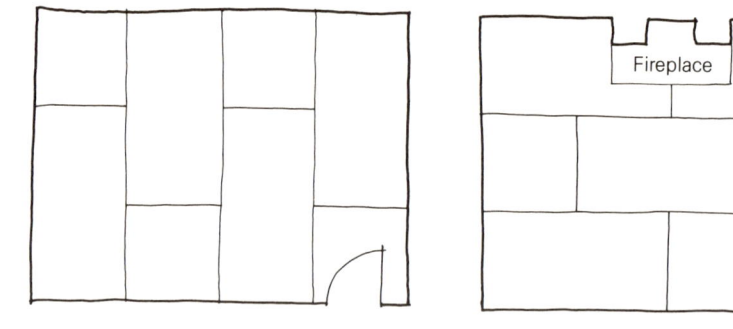

Hardboard is relatively cheap, comes in a range of warm woody colours and looks good on its own (with a rug or two) as well as being an essential base for most sheet and tile flooring. Get tempered hardboard.

1. Preparation. Knock in nails ¼ inch (6mm) below the wood surface and take out all tacks, etc. Ideally the floor boards should be as smooth and even as possible. You can sand them down or plane them level where necessary.

2. Plan how you will lay the panels. Most usual size is 8ft x 4ft (2.4m x 1.2m) and is best used uncut except at edges. The diagram shows how you can centre them on a floor. Try and use the panels to help the shape of the room. In a narrow room put them longways across the width of the room.

3. For difficult projections, make a template as a guide for cutting.

4. Lay the hardboard rough side down and fix with panel pins at 6 inch (15cm) centres around the edges of each panel. If the hardboard is to act as a sub-floor to another finish, the panel pins should go right across at 6 inch (15cm) intervals like a dot-to-dot crossword.

5. Seal with polyurethane seal (Ronseal, etc.).

6. There are other wood finishes which you can also lay yourself. They are more expensive than hardboard but look very good for years — hardboard really only looks its best for five years. They are also harder to cut to shape when necessary. JL has used 2 foot (60cm) squares of birch-faced ply. Par-K-Ply gives the effect of parquet.

Floor treatments — laying sheet vinyl and foam backed carpet

These are floor coverings we have frequently suggested because they are not too expensive and easy to lay. You can cut them with a Stanley knife, and as many come in widths around 12ft (3.6m) you need have no problems with seams. What's more you can pick them up off the floor and take them with you when you move.

1. Prepare the floor as above. The sheet flooring can be laid over other level sub-floors (and finishes) if they are free from damp. They can also be laid direct over concrete if this is dry.

2. Cut very roughly to shape and put it down on the floor for a week before cutting it finally to shape and fixing it.

3. To cut to shape make a template from newspaper or brown paper. Sellotape this on to the vinyl or carpet. Cut round with a Stanley knife.

4. Don't stick them down whatever instructions say. Fix vinyl to wood floors with panel pins and use double-sided tape on concrete. Fix carpet down with double-sided adhesive tape to either floor. (If you glue them down, you will find it difficult if not impossible to get them up without tearing up half the original floor!) Lay hardboard sub-floor where base is uneven.

Making your own curtains

Thanks to Rufflette tapes, making curtains is a matter of sewing straight seams on the straight of the material, if to begin with you can deny yourself flounces and frills.

1. Almost any material is suitable for curtains. Curtains made with generous amounts of inexpensive fabric can look a great deal more opulent than curtains made from insufficient fabric however grand. We suggest you start on a small-scale by making curtains from material that is easy to handle (cotton or linen) and for windows which are not too large.

2. The Rufflette Regis tape gives you very professional-looking, even pencil pleating. The curtain head can then either conceal the track or it can be mounted on to a plain wood pole with rings. (Rufflette Hi-style does the same thing for lightweight fabrics.) If you use these tapes you need material measuring twice the length of your track.

3. We use the sewing machine for sewing on the tape and joining, when necessary, widths of material. Both these and the side seams will pucker less if you snip the selvedges through every 6 in (15cm).

4. Start with a fabric which does not need careful matching. When you use a big pattern, it is essential to match it up, which is extremely hard if the pattern is not printed square onto the fabric. You must start square on the fabric (not the pattern — if it is too askew, take the fabric back to the shop!) then carefully match at the seams.

5. The side seams at each edge sit better if you tack or pin and press them down first, then sew by hand. Before hemming the bottom let the curtains hang for a few weeks (don't wait until the pins go rusty) then hem by hand.

6. Put borders on by hand. You can do borders at the side before hanging, but bottom borders only when you have set the hem.

7. Linings in grand curtains are sewn to the curtain, interlined with layers of lovely stuff called bumf! Simpler linings are made using an insulating curtain lining itself coated with aluminium called Milium, with a Rufflette Lining tape. This makes an independent lining which you hook on to the same hooks as the curtain. It helps the curtain fall as well as reflecting the heat back into the room.

8. When making net curtains use the finest polyester thread; don't bother with side seams but give them a double hem to help them hang. Instead of curtain track you can mount them on a natural or painted wood, brass or chrome pole, allowing as much material as possible in the width.

9. When you become more ambitious, there are lots of books and brochures showing how to vary your curtains. One recent one full of ideas is Tricia Guild's *Soft Furnishing* which takes you into the area of decorative cushions, tablecloths and lampshades, upholstery and bedspreads as well as curtains.

10. If you can make curtains, you can make blinds. Start with a kit for a roller blind. Then, when you've found out the snags for yourself, you can choose your own material, treat it to become stiff and experiment with different styles at the bottom. Roman blinds look madly grand but need a lot of care.

Five ways to improve insulation

1. The roof. See Chapter 4 page 45. Once you have access to the roof space, which we consider essential, you can fill between and over the joists with glass-fibre blanket, as thick as you like, providing you keep extra moisture from the room below out as we suggest.

2. You can line the underside of the roof itself with agricultural polythene (very thick quality) to stop draughts whistling in through gaps in the tiles. Hire a commercial stapler to fix the polythene, because with this you won't jog the tiles loose as you would by hammering. Leave some gaps so that gentle ventilation allows any condensation or moisture to evaporate.

3. Put draught excluders on all outside doors and windows if they fit badly. Good D-I-Y shops and builders merchants will advise. The new Berger Silicone self-moulding draught seal will adapt to any type of gap.

4. Where you will not want to open windows, put up some D-I-Y double-glazing which you can fix in place all winter and remove for the summer if you need to.

JL is very pleased with her Grippa Frame which is tough plastic but looks like traditional wood window mouldings and can be attached either inside or outside the window frame. For heat insulation the optimum is 2-4 in (5-10cm) between the panes and even this will help with sound. (Aim for 4-8 in (10-20cm) where noise is a real problem.) You can use acrylic sheet which is lighter to handle than glass.

5. You lose a lot of heat from the hot water cylinder if you rely on ready-made insulation jackets. If you want an airing cupboard, the hot pipes into and out of the cylinder should heat a small space sufficiently. To insulate the cylinder properly you need to construct a box around it with plywood or hardboard — the walls of the airing cupboard can provide two or three of the sides — and fill the space between the sides and the cylinder with Kapok (glass-fibre blanket has little filaments which would irritate your skin if they got into your clothes or linen). Make a

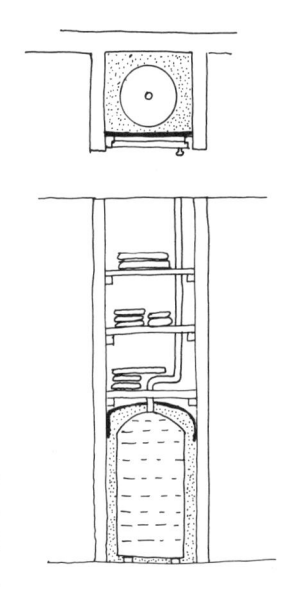

Figure 24. *Airing Cupboards*. Don't be content with a shop-bought insulating jacket for your hot water cylinder. Box it in with hardboard or plywood and then pack with loose cotton flock, protecting the top with linen or cotton tucked well down the sides. The emerging pipes at the top will give adequate heat for airing clothes.

'lid' of cloth or polythene which can be tucked down into the sides and tied around the pipes at the top. See the diagram. If you do this to your cylinder, you will find that it even becomes economic to use an immersion heater!

Fixing shelving, units and curtain rails to walls

A lot of your own efforts at economy are wasted if you have to pay someone else to come in and fix up your curtain rails or shelving.

1. Invest in a basic drill such as a Black and Decker. You will find it useful for all sorts of D-I-Y projects and it is a much more efficient way to drill your initial holes than chipping away inexpertly with a cold chisel.

2. All aspects of fixing are covered in detail by the *Reader's Digest* D-I-Y manual in the 'Fixing and Fastening' section. Rawlplug also have very good instructions about which Rawlplug to use on what wall.

3. You have to be sure whether you are trying to fix something on to a solid wall or a hollow one. Solid walls are brick, stone, or block, with concrete lintels over window frames in newer houses. Hollow (stud) walls are inside walls where plasterboard (or in old houses the laths and plaster) is supported by vertical and horizontal timber framing set at approximately 2ft (60cm) intervals. The Rawlplugs you use will depend on which kind of wall you are fixing to.

4. When fixing battens to a solid wall (to take cupboards or units or curtain rails), you have some leeway where you will actually make the fixing. Finding the vertical stud in hollow walls is a matter of practice. Some people can tell by banging the wall and detecting the sound-change where there is a stud. Others poke with a bradawl and then fill in the holes later. After you have located one, the next ones are usually about 2ft(60cm) on either side.

5. Fixing up adjustable shelving (such as Tebrax or Spur systems) is a little more tricky because (see diagram) you have to get the verticals the right distances from each other in relation to the ultimate length of the shelves. So in some cases where the studs are not conveniently placed, you may not be able to get your shelves spanning the whole width you want. It is very important to get the vertical supports truly vertical — use a plumb-line. And the shelves truly horizontal — use a spirit level.

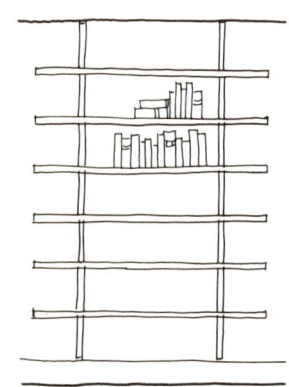

Figure 25. *Adjustable Shelving Systems.* Shelves should never span more than 900mm centre to centre and never overlap at free ends more than one-fifth of the supported span. With stud walls (wood framing behind plaster) locate the studs and attach the upright tracks to these.

6. Shelves for these systems remain stable using ¾ inch (20cm) blockboard rather than planks which may be more expensive and can warp. Sand and stain or seal them or paint them. Cover the three exposed edges with ¼ inch × ¾ inch (6mm × 18mm) flat softwood trim pinned and glued in position.

Ceramic tiles

The D-I-Y supermarkets and departments are full of these tiles with the right adhesives, groutings and tools. They are expensive to have fixed, but affordable in small quantities if you do them yourself, e.g. along the edges of bath and basin, the work surface in the kitchen, even up the walls of a shower.

1. To begin with, select a firm level wall to put tiles on. Any wall or floor can be tiled, but these both need special preparation to get the surface firm and level.

2. Choose modern tiles which are not too difficult to cut and have their own spacers so you get the exact distance between the tiles correctly. The *Reader's Digest* manual has another excellent section on ceramic tiling. Get all the tools and adhesives and grouting necessary at the same time.

3. Setting out the tiles properly is important. Where the tiles run the length of a wall, start at the centre and work out to the edges. Along the bath, start at the free edge and work towards the corner. If both ends are free, centre and overlap no more than ⅛ inch at each end. From a window sill work down to a work surface or vanitory unit. Fill any gap at the bottom with a softwood batten. Do the same under kitchen wall cupboards.

4. Grouting is the final touch which gives a professional look.

5. For showers, use a quarter circle section of tile bedded in Dow Corning mastic to complete the joint between the ceramic tray and tiles. This will throw the water off the joint and help keep it waterproof.

Figure 26. *Fixing Ceramic Tiles.* Try to avoid cutting tiles horizontally and infill the gap left below with painted or sealed wood battens or upstands matching the work-top. Cut them vertically when necessary at corners. Centring them where there are corners at both ends of the tiled area, always starting with a full tile where one end is free.

14 Planning your housekeeping

> 'He solemnly conjured me, I remember, to take warning by his fate; and to observe that if a man had twenty pounds a year for his income, and spent nineteen pounds nineteen shillings and sixpence, he would be happy, but that if he spent twenty pounds one, he would be miserable'
>
> MR. MICAWBER

> 'The value of money is one of the first things every woman should learn ... as the basis of all good housekeeping lies in the proper control of the purse'
>
> THE WOMEN'S BOOK, Ed. Florence B. Jack, 1911

Housekeeping, in Roget's *Thesaurus*, is referred to under 'Management', which puts it into its right category. There is no way we can generalise about your budgeting or cash-flow here. But whatever you have to spend, whether it is riches or something between a modest amount and practically nothing, you will want to get value for money. So in this chapter we are going to discuss some steps you can take to make sure you do get value — whether you're buying something important for the house, doing your weekly shopping or entertaining friends — and how to set about getting credit to pay for it when necessary.

The major shopping

When you set up house for the first time you embark on shopping on a whole new scale. Furniture, appliances, fabrics, fittings — you need to make decisions about a lot of things that have to last you a long time if they are going to repay your investment. How can you be sure you are making a good buy?

Don't rush into things — do your research

1. A visit to the Design Centre and/or a study of the Design Index

is useful because the goods have been pre-selected for you. Selection committees set up by the Design Council choose British goods for functional efficiency, ease of maintenance, ease of manufacture, value for money and good appearance. They take advice from outside organisations on such things as functional efficiency. Some of the things selected are on view at the Design Centre in the Haymarket, London. All of them (about 10,000) are on the Design Index, which you can study yourself at the Design Centre in London or the one in Glasgow. The Index is a gold mine of information because it covers almost every household need (from floors to fabrics, kitchen appliances to bath taps, chairs to chopping boards). It is kept up to date as far as possible with photographs or samples and prices. It is a good way of compiling a short list of choices among British goods. It does not help you through the maze of imports except that you have something to compare them against.

2. Looking at the relevant copies of *Which?* will also help you build-up short-lists. *Which?* is the magazine published by the Consumers' Association. The aim of the CA is to give people factual, independent and objective information. *Which?* contains reports on goods and services on everything from electric toothbrushes to packaged holidays, if possible giving in each case your Best Buy. You may not always agree with the priorities used to decide on the Best Buy. And often the survey is a bit out-of-date by the time you want to consult it. But the tests it carries out do help you have some criteria to measure your purchases against. This is very useful when you start having to buy expensive things which you have not previously thought about much.

You get hold of copies of *Which?* from your public library (usually the reference section so you can't take them home). Or, if you're public spirited and want to support the CA, which is independent and unsubsidised, you become a CA member and receive a copy each month. The CA, incidentally, also publishes a lot of extremely informative books which take you intelligently from the cradle (with *The Newborn Baby*) to the grave (*What to do When Someone Dies*) with several in between on buying a house and setting up home. These are available from enlightened booksellers or the CA itself.

3. Make a point of reading the magazines and sections of newspapers, not to mention books, which are discussing your very problems. Journalists are doing a lot of your preliminary legwork — finding out about and reacting to products and ideas. Don't neglect the ads, because if you send off the little coupons you can get back brochures, full of information, prices and stockists.

4. There are still a few shops where the buyer, if not the assistants, actually can tell you about the products on sale — which are value for money and why. If you find a shop like this use it. You'll get the best out of the staff if you go at quiet times (i.e. not Saturday morning).

5. Check after-sales service especially if you are buying anything electronic, electrical or mechanical. Only friends living in the same district can give you real insight gained from experience — whether the man to service the boiler keeps his appointments, whether you can actually get through to the washing machine manufacturer's service number let alone get an appointment. Some imported domestic appliances which seem excellent buys fall down on service — especially if you live a long way from their main importer.

Picking things up cheap

If you do your research, you give yourself a choice: you can either get the particular piece of furniture or appliance at the most convenient shop at its recommended price, brand new and hopefully in good working order — or you are well enough informed to pick up a bargain if you see one. When setting up house few of us have the money to buy everything we'd like to from Harrods. We have to decide which things we really must spend the money we've got on and then, for the rest, we have to improvise. If you look around you'll understand how some people really do manage never to pay the full price for anything.

1. Branded appliances, units, furniture etc. are nearly always cheaper in discount stores or superstores (like ASDA, Comet or Carrefour). As some of these only give minimal service on the shop-floor, you have to know exactly the brand and model you want before you go. Other places offer branded goods at cut prices during the sales, which recently have been really worthwhile. Or when the end of a line is being sold off. Sometimes a store like John Lewis buys up a model which has been superseded — and it's seldom much different from the new model except in price.

2. 'Own Brand' appliances, like the Electra electrical equipment and appliances marketed by the electricity boards (many of which are made by the same manufacturers as make the branded goods) look very similar to branded appliances but are cheaper. The wide range of Jonelle goods (at John Lewis stores) and the smaller range of St Michael household things (Marks & Spencer) are also good buys.

3. Ads in local papers, garage sales and so on. A lot of people have things to sell (the unwanted-gift, the going-abroad syndrome). If you know what you want, the small ads are rewarding. A friend of ours bought eight Bauhaus armchairs for half their new cost through the local paper. SK, reluctantly about to spend nearly £300 on a big new fridge, picked up a bargain for £70 from a family whose kitchen was changing colour from white to brown. You gamble a bit, but your outlay is usually much smaller. Check real age, instructions, guarantee, service arrangements, etc.

4. Reconditioned appliances — for example, cookers and sewing machines are often good value because there is usually a short guarantee. These are getting rarer because the real price of most new appliances has come down. They have also become more complex so it is often not worth anyone's while to take the time and trouble. Reconditioned good quality pianos are still often better value than new ones.

5. Secondhand stores, 'antique' markets. Good bets for furniture but not usually appliances. The less smart they are the better the bargains. The more ingenious and clever you are at doing-up things, the more it's worth your while.

6. Auctions and sales. Like the small ads, you may or may not find just what you want. If you'd like to buy at auctions but have never tried, start by going along to the regular sales the chief auctioneers hold in your area and see how they work. If you feel confident enough to buy, make sure you go to 'viewing day', usually the day before. Also before you get carried away by the excitement of the moment, mark what you are prepared to pay in your catalogue. Bidding is simple at this level — there is no substitute for shouting out your bid. This attracts the attention of the auctioneer. He knows you're in the running so then looks at you to see if you want to bid up. If so, you nod your head and the price goes up automatically in the £1, £10 or £50 jumps it has been going up. If you want to change the amount by which you are raising your bid, you will have to shout out your next price. To stop bidding, shake your head at the auctioneer when he next looks at you. JL found she could confidently bid for cottages after a few initial runs with Victorian jewelcases and a set of Windsor kitchen chairs.

You can leave bids with the doorman, but this is not the way to get a real bargain.

If your bid succeeds, remember that you are expected to pay straight away. You are also responsible for taking away what you've bought.

It's tricky buying appliances at auctions. The catalogue seldom commits itself to promising 'perfect working order'. There is one London saleroom which earned a weekly commission on a bargain vacuum cleaner. It was the wrong voltage. So, as buyer after buyer just commissioned the auctioneer to re-sell it at the next week's auction, he earned a weekly commission on it.

Getting some credit
Bargains and credit don't really go together! But you can spread the cost of major purchases by getting credit in one form or another.

In times of inflation, buying on credit is often more sensible than saving up — simply because it is hardly possible to keep the value of cash in step with inflation. But you must try to get credit on the most advantageous terms for yourself. This has been made easier since October 1980 when all advertisements or literature offering credit by law have to quote the true interest rate (or APR — the Annual Percentage Rate). This helps you sort out whether 18.5% from your bank is cheaper or more expensive than 20% deposit and monthly payments of £15 over 2 years. If the APR is not quoted you are entitled to ask for it in writing.

If you plan to use credit, you will find it worth while to keep up a good credit record. First, by not taking on more commitments than you can pay off. Second, by managing your finances in a businesslike way. You will often be asked for references — from your bank, your employer or places where you have accounts (if you want to open a new one). If you have a good record with your bank, or with any previous commitments, you will find it comparatively simple to get credit. There are credit-reference agencies which sound alarming, but only are if you get in their bad books. In any case, if you are refused credit you have the right to demand why, to ask the credit reference agency for a copy of their file and, if it is incorrect, to insist on it being corrected.

Today, loans ear-marked for home improvements can qualify for tax relief on the interest. Home improvements are defined as things which alter a home permanently. Repairs don't count, nor buying things which are not fixtures. So converting your loft, re-vamping the kitchen with fitted units, installing insulation and central heating, even putting in a swimming pool all count.

Here are some sources of credit which are worth investigating:

1. Banks. For many years restricted in their ability/desire to lend by current governments. Now anxious not only for your account, but also to lend to good customers.

Overdrafts are generally considered the cheapest and most flexible way to borrow money. Negotiate with your own manager. Rates of interest may vary. There is no tax relief even if the money goes on home improvements.

Ordinary loans are more formal than overdrafts, but are also negotiated with the manager. Can be for home-improvements with tax concession.

Personal loans involve a fixed sum, fixed interest and fixed time to pay back. Negotiate with bank manager. Can be for home-improvements with tax concession.

2. Credit cards — like Access and Barclaycard. Anyone over eighteen can apply for one, and your credit limit will be related to your job, income, etc.

If you buy things on credit cards, you pay no interest if you settle the bill within a month. But the interest mounts up if you let your debt run.

If you want to spend more than you can repay in three months, you would probably be better off with an Access loan or a Barclay Masterloan. They send you details with their bills whether you ask or not. You apply by filling in the application form. There is no tax relief on the interest even if the loan is used for home improvements.

3. Building society. As an addition to your mortgage or for home improvements, if your income allows. These qualify for tax relief on interest. See your local branch manager. Alternatives such as increasing your mortgage or taking on a second mortgage are not really advisable for first-time buyers, except to do up a property that was cheap and that you intend to stay in for some time — at least five years.

4. Insurance policy loans. If you have a whole life policy or an endowment policy you can negotiate a loan of (usually) up to 90% of the current cash-in value with the insurance company whose policy you hold. You only pay interest on the loan, but the amount is taken out of what you get from the policy when it matures. This is a cheap way of getting a loan if you already have a policy. Could get you tax relief on interest if used for home-improvements..

5. Hire purchase. Usually arranged by the shop where you buy, but the cash is actually lent by a finance company. You have to pay a deposit. Notice the interest rate. The fiction is that you are hiring the goods until you've finished paying for them. Unless any defect is pointed out in the agreement, the goods have to be in proper working order, so the shop has to put right any defects and provide a substitute while they do.

You can give back the goods and end the agreement, but will have to pay a minimum of half the total cost. The shop or finance company can repossess the goods if you fall behind with your payments — but they are usually willing to accommodate you if you ask them, by giving you extra time to pay.

Keep your copy of any HP agreement carefully as you will have to know the name of the finance company as well as the shop. If you sign an HP agreement in your own home, you have the additional protection of the three-day 'cooling-off' period during which you can call off the deal.

6. Credit sales. This is offered by shops and is very similar to HP. You pay in installments, but you own the goods from the start. This means that you cannot decide to give back the things half-way through but you can, on the other hand, sell them. If you do, you have to pay back the shop (or rather the finance company) the full amount you owe them.

7. Finance company loans. These are usually offered on big purchases — like cars — either by the shop or a finance company directly. You can locate an individual finance company by writing to the Finance Houses Association. These loans are more like personal loans in that you are lent the money to buy the goods, and you pay back the lender as agreed. Interest-rates are usually higher than a bank's. Be careful if you are asked also to take out an insurance policy as security. Could get you tax-relief if used for home improvements.

8. Credit from particular shops. Some shops offer budget accounts, monthly accounts or option accounts. Like credit cards these save money if you pay them off regularly (monthly), but the interest can mount up if you have an outstanding debt. Their advantage is convenience and credit for a short time, while you arrange a longer term way of paying.

9. Credit from mail order. When you order by mail from an ad you usually have to send money or your Access/Barclaycard number. But if you order from one of the big mail order catalogues you can usually spread your payments over twenty weeks or more without paying any interest.

10. Trading checks or vouchers. Tallymen. Moneylenders. Pawnbrokers. Avoid if at all possible. Every survey shows they cost more, because you pay higher rates of interest (all) or your choice is restricted (trading checks and vouchers) or the terms are seldom clearly set out in writing (Tallymen).

Your rights as a consumer

These have been extended a lot during the past twenty-five years. First, however, before you get militant and suspicious, remember that it is in the shop's interest and the manufacturer's to have a satisfied customer. Although people and firms who rip you off do exist, there are many more trying to make a decent living for themselves. There are two things they offer, which do not affect your legal rights:

a. Guarantees. These come with almost all appliances, most furniture, some kitchen equipment (even some saucepans). Fill them in and send them back and keep a record — so you have something to quote if necessary. Keep the original shop bill too. Guarantees do not affect your rights under the Sale of Goods Act (see below). If something you have bought is demonstrably faulty, or breaks down within the period of the guarantee — take it back to the shop even though the guarantee is given by the manufacturer. The shop may replace it straight away, or send it back to the manufacturer for repair under the guarantee. Only if you can't get to the shop, should you contact the manufacturer direct. SK was rewarded when her freezer broke down one Christmas Eve by the shop miraculously finding the record of her having bought it, and therefore the repair (an expensive new compressor) was done free of charge under the guarantee.

b. Trade Associations. These have been formed by groups of traders or retailers to protect themselves, but as they are anxious to give their whole trade a good name, they act informally to help consumers in difficulty with one of their members. (They are not nearly so formalised as the professional associations, like the RIBA for architects, but do give you an indication of their members' good faith.) Associations range from the National Bedding Federation to the British Carpet Manufacturers' Association, from the Dishwasher Council to the Heating and Ventilating Contractors. The Electrical Association for Women (25 Foubert Place, London W.1.) will give unbiased advice on the selection of electrical appliances.

Second, there are several organisations which set independent standards. For example, the British Standards Institute sets standards for a wide range of things (including the colours as discussed on page 61) which, if they live up to the standard agreed on, have the kite mark and the BS reference. Some have the additional BSI Safety Mark.

The Gas Council insists that all gas appliances sold through Gas Board outlets should reach the BSI standards of safety and they will also carry the Gas Council's Seal of Approval. Electrical appliances with the British Electro Technical Approvals Board label have been independently tested. It is compulsory for electric blankets to carry the BEAB label. All these labels are a guarantee of performance.

The Solid Fuel Advisory Service publishes annually a list of approved appliances giving details of function and output.

These are all voluntary efforts to ensure proper standards. If they fail or you strike unlucky, you have been given certain rights by law. And a great consumer protection industry has also arisen to support you.

As long ago as 1893 the Sale of Goods Act obliged a shop to carry out what it had promised. When you pay your money and the shop hands over the goods, it has by this contract made itself responsible for the quality and fitness of the goods for the purpose they have been sold. Since the 1960s your rights have been strengthened by legislation — or at least shops can be prosecuted for false descriptions, dodging liability for negligence, taking away your rights with exclusion clauses in small print. There is control over credit — the compulsion to disclose the APR (see above) for instance. Standards in hygiene and labelling of food products are also laid down.

These laws and their implications for you are discussed very readably in a book based on the Thames TV programme, *Money Go Round* (*Buy Right* by Mary McAnnally and Rosemary Delbridge).

Hopefully, if you buy faulty appliances, your initial complaint to the shop will put the matter right. There are, however, techniques for complaining:

1. Make your complaint as soon as possible after you discover the fault.

2. If you can, take the faulty goods back to the shop, and calmly and politely explain what is wrong. Take with you your bill, guarantee, etc., leave photocopies if you like, but keep the originals. If you can't take it (because it's a washing machine or a cooker, for example) then still go in person with all the documents.

3. If you first of all have to explain to an assistant, be prepared to explain, just as calmly, all over again to the responsible person — the owner, or the buyer (in a department store) or the manager (in a chain store or supermarket).

4. If you can't go, telephone. Or, write a letter (and keep a copy) giving the facts as concisely as possible and say whether you want a replacement or a repair. Send copies if possible of the original bill. Write to the top person: if in doubt managing director is as good a title as any. (Don't, as a friend of ours did once, write to somebody at the top known to you personally and intersperse your complaint with tender enquiries about his mistress.)

If by great misfortune you come up against a firm which is as intransigent as the washing machine manufacturer the late Kenneth Allsop had to pursue, or the villainous firms revealed on radio by investigators like Roger Cook or programmes like *You and Yours*, take advice from experts. The nearest Citizen's Advice Bureau (there are now over 800) is your best bet. They can advise you on your next step, who to approach and how, and if necessary how to go about getting legal advice. It's a lot cheaper than rushing off to your solicitor, who will charge for every minute of his time.

SETTING UP HOME

Day to day shopping v the weekly expedition

Managing the weekly shopping is rather different. For one thing, unless you've spent your life in deprivation at a boarding school, you're familiar with most of what you buy.

But most of us spend quite a chunk of our income on this part of 'the housekeeping'. From figures in the government-produced Family Expenditure Survey, it seems that, on average, each household spends about 25% of its income on food and household things. This is as much as most building societies reckon you should be spending on your mortgage repayments! So it is just as important to get value for money.

Thanks to a number of fairly recent laws (the Food and Drugs Act of 1955, the Weights and Measures Act of 1963, the Trade Descriptions Act of 1968) you are protected from grossly bad buys like food unfit for human consumption, misleading information and packaging. (These are explained in *Buy Right*, mentioned above.) The onus of actually prosecuting traders/manufacturers under these laws is on the local authority. But things very often come to light only if you play your part, which is to report any infringements affecting you to the Trading Standards Officer or the Environmental Health Officer at your local authority.

The big question for most of us is — how far is it worth shopping around for lower prices? You have to set money-saved eventually against time, plus any costs you incur travelling. We think the shopping in a neighbourhood is very important when you are choosing your house (see page 28). Obviously the systematic shopper who makes a weekly or monthly list and knows what favourite brands cost will score. But some things are better bought fresh — bread, cheese, cold meats, fresh fruit, salads and vegetables, and meat from a good butcher. And for these a good source near your home (or work if you have some way of getting it home easily) is a great advantage and an economy in the long run. Here are some of our personal findings in our ever-lasting quests for value for money:

Cash-and-carry stores

These are the wholesale outlets where shops, restaurants and small catering establishments replenish their supplies. The prices stagger one — they are so much lower! Packs are huge or you have to buy goods in trays of twelve upwards, so it is only sensible to get brands you know and love!

The problem is that entry is restricted to trade only and you have to have a card. We mention this source in case you have any connections who legitimately have a card. If so, use them!

Supermarkets
Most of us have to rely on these to get lower prices. The bigger the chain, the lower, usually, the prices because they can benefit most from manufacturers' discounts. You can take advantage of their special offers which will be even cheaper. The supermarket's 'own brands' are always cheaper than the equivalent brand but only worth buying if you like them as much. Big packs are only cheaper if you can use them up before they go off!
From experience, small and medium-size branches are often frustrating to shop in because they don't carry all the alternative lines or the larger more economical-sized packs.

Freezer centres
These seem often to give very good value with own brands and huge packs. Some good frozen brands do 'freezer' packs which work out cheaper fish finger for fish finger than the normal packs. Be cautious and test the quality with small packs of the freezer centre's own brands, especially if your freezer space is limited, before you allow yourself to be carried away to buy a car-load of frozen white elephants. There's a big snag, we find, about those attractive-sounding 'sides of beef' because it often turns out that there is a lot of the 'side' that you normally don't want to cook or eat. Small freezer centres offer large packs but not invariably small prices. Freezer centres attached to a farm where they sell their own meat are excellent value very often, but not in the sense that the meat is cheap. It is just very good meat, well-butchered, etc.

P-Y-O fruit and veg
(*Pick Your Own — from the field where it is grown*). Wonderful value especially if you go before many other eager pickers plus their small children have vandalised the crop. You get to know the best local places and days to go. Some advertise locally, but the best tips are from local people. There is even a special P-Y-O magazine listing farms, etc. It's especially good if you have freezer capacity and therefore can freeze and use the produce

SETTING UP HOME

when it's otherwise out of season. It is very hard just to pick enough for two for one weekend. If you really want to economise you must cost your time and travelling. (Driving the fifty miles from London to Haslemere, as a friend of ours did for P-Y-O raspberries, needs quite a bit of justification!)

Markets
Nearly every town has a market someplace where stalls sell mainly fruit and veg, but sometimes also fish, dairy products and meat. If you like the haggle and bustle and challenge of markets, they are fun to shop at and you get things in season at what seem low prices. Sometimes it's true the price is low because some of what you buy is not in prime condition. However most market stalls provide a regular livelihood to their owners who are there every day or every week, so if you go often you can get to know which ones have good produce and real bargains.

Use your initiative
If you shop regularly so you get to know the manager or owner of a shop, you can approach him for a special price if you buy in bulk. SK has done this with catfood and saved an appreciable amount per tin. But even as little as 5% adds up over the year. Greengrocers also have been persuaded to sell us whole trays of fruit at a discount. The good butcher round the corner will butcher the side of beef and do it so that you can use all of it! It may not be quite as cheap as the price of the ready-butchered side, but it will be cheaper than buying the meat day-by-day.

There are just two things to bear in mind before you buy in bulk anywhere:

1. You have to store the stuff somewhere. Household things and dry goods need dry cupboard space with cleaning things separate from edible food. Fresh produce (to be kept several days) needs a cool ventilated place but not necessarily a fridge. If you are going to freeze or buy frozen things in bulk, you need enough freezer space or a friend with more than enough.

2. If you are on a weekly budget, and you shop in bulk monthly — or suddenly swoop on a particularly good farm shop — you need to adjust your weekly spending accordingly. Seems obvious, but SK often forgets this!

A new approach to food

There's one thing that sometimes gets forgotten as you shop around for bargain packs and frozen goodies, heave it all home and stash it away. This is the ultimate purpose of the activity as far as shopping for food is concerned. You are not just re-fuelling yourself for another week. You are also keeping yourself healthy. More than that, the food you eat and the way you serve it is an important part of the way you live. It should give you pleasure rather than be a penance.

Keeping yourself healthy
It is surprising to learn that over 40% of the recruits for the Boer War were rejected as unfit. Even at the time (early years of this century) the middle class civil servants were sufficiently appalled to set up a committee of enquiry. They came to the conclusion that poverty, and the malnutrition resulting from it, were to blame.

Since that time the pendulum has swung the other way so that today we are increasingly at risk from the so-called 'diseases of affluence'. In other words we have too much to eat — or too much of certain foods. Obesity has been called the most common nutritional disorder in Britain today and is an important medical problem contributing to the incidence of diabetes, coronary artery disease, gall-bladder disease and varicose veins. Other related diseases include coronary heart disease, certain diseases of the large intestine (including appendicitis and cancer) and bad teeth.

This means that today we have to select what we eat more intelligently from a very wide choice. Perhaps it seems a bit ridiculous to think about your health in late middle age before you are thirty, but, first, bad eating habits are hard to break, so you may as well start now. Second, if and when you are pregnant, what you eat and how well you are, directly affect the health of your baby. Third, you pass your eating habits (good and bad) on to your children and this directly affects their whole lives.

The choice to make and the eating habits to develop are not always easy to disentangle from the fads and newsflashes about diet that get most publicity. Unfortunately nutritionists resemble economists (only more so) in that if you put three of them in a room together they come out with five (rather than three) solutions. However, some guiding thoughts emerge:

It is important to have a varied diet. If you do you will almost automatically get all the carbohydrates, proteins, fats, vitamins and minerals your body needs. (If you want to know more about nutrition, we recommend one short book out of hundreds as a starter: *Eating for Health* produced by the Department of Health and Social Security. If you don't want to trudge and wait at a government bookshop, you can get a bookshop to order it for you.)

Vegetarians can eat a satisfactory and varied diet, especially if they consume eggs and dairy products. Vegans, who take only vegetable foods, have to be more careful. The diets that can be dangerous are those which are very restricted — the sort of faddy eating a dieting teenager might decide to stick to.

How much food you should eat depends on your individual metabolism and the energy you expend through your day. Your basal metabolic rate is the energy (or calories) you use just existing. For instance, it has been calculated that a woman weighing 55 kg. uses 54 calories an hour or 1250-plus a day. That's before you start running for buses, rushing round shops and going to meetings.

The amount of food you need can be calculated so that you have enough to keep you at just the right weight. Tables have generally been calculated from life insurance statistics, so these are a good source to check yourself against. Obviously if you are over-weight you have to eat less. SK found a suitably slim paperback called *The New Calorie Counter* by Lorraine Hunter interesting and helpful, and worth studying before rushing out masochistically to follow diets like Dr. Atkins' Revolutionary Diet or Dr. Tarnower's Scarsdale Diet.

Some foods are considered to be less satisfactory sources of nourishment than others. Professor Yudkin has led a long campaign to point out the dangers of too much highly-refined sugar in the diet of this country. Sugar gives you a lot of calories, very little other nourishment, and is addictive. You get a 'sweet tooth'. You put on weight without noticing. (A horrid thought is that you have to walk a mile to eat off the effect of a mere four to five lumps of sugar.)

In Britain our sugar consumption, though declining slightly, is still one of the highest per head in the world. If you want sweet things, follow the lead of cuisine minceur and use a sugar substitute. Saccharin, although from time to time found fatal for rats in very high doses, is the most useful because it contributes sweetness but no calories. Cyclamates are banned in a number of countries. Sorbitol is used instead of sugar for diabetics, but unfortunately has almost the same number of calories as sugar teaspoon for teaspoon.

Other carbohydrates, potatoes for example and wholemeal bread, are coming in out of the cold. Not only because they provide other vitamins and minerals, but also because they provide important dietary fibres and some protein. *The McGovern Report on Dietary Goals for the USA*, while advising sugar consumption be reduced, felt carbohydrate consumption should be increased to account for 40-45% energy intake.

There is a certain amount of controversy over fats. Fats make food much tastier and include all the delicious dairy produce like cream, butter, Jersey milk, full-cream yoghourt, cheese, etc. The same *McGovern Report* recommended that fats should supply only 30% of energy intake (instead of 42%).

In Britain we have been consuming greater and greater quantities of fats since the 1950s and the latest figures show that in this country as a whole we are now getting equal amounts of energy from fats and carbohydrates. Does this matter? Some medical opinion believes there is a link between diet and coronary heart disease and has been recommending since 1974 that the amount of saturated fat (from plant and animal sources) in the diet should be reduced. So where an alternative is possible it is a good idea to use a polyunsaturated fat (spreads like Gold or Flora instead of margarine, or fry in oil from sunflower, corn or blends labelled as polyunsaturated).

Fresh foods — fruit and vegetables — are extremely good, and nobody has yet said a word against them. But if they have begun to wilt, they have begun to lose their valuable vitamin C. (Also with the recent revelations about the effects of lead and the way it is being distributed by cars and lorries' exhaust, one begins to wonder about the value of fruit and vegetables grown by busy roads or exposed in traffic-congested high-streets.)

There is much prejudice about preserved and processed foods. But freezing affects produce so little that vegetables are really equivalent to fresh. (Those commercials about picking peas the moment they are perfect are based on truth!) Fish is probably fresher than the stuff that used to trundle down in melting ice from Grimsby. If you cook frozen food as instructed, you will lose the minimum nutrients.

The much-maligned white sliced loaf has its full complement of B vitamins (the ones lost in the high extraction rate of white flour) added plus extra calcium. Margarine has added vitamin A and D so nutritionally it is the equal of butter (in fact some brands could be said to be better as they are made from polyunsaturated fat!) Other processed foods have added vitamins so it is worth choosing the brands that do.

We do all have to accept modern technology in food processing if we are going to live in towns, shop in supermarkets and spend less time preparing and cooking food.

Putting all this into practice
There is no one magic way of putting all this into practice — no specific régime to follow which would apply to everyone's individual needs. You must always remember that there are no absolutes. One reason is that nutritionists could never agree about what a healthy diet would consist of in more detail. A second is that medical research is continually making new discoveries about the way our bodies react to food — which in any case is only one among many factors affecting health. (The others being such immovables as family, heredity, environment, as well as the problems and stresses of everyday life.)

Our feeling is that you just have to take your present pattern of eating, shopping and cooking and adapt it a little, with healthy eating in mind.

Are health foods the answer? For some people they are. Health food shops concentrate on a wide variety of whole cereals and grains, dried fruit and nuts, familiar and unfamiliar pulses, foods grown without the use of chemical fertilizers and pesticides. Free range eggs of course. Honey. Wholemeal bread. (But no meat, fish or broiler chickens!) The idea that food should be wholesome, real and unpolluted is very attractive and harks back to a pleasant farmhouse way of life centred round the kitchen table and the open fire. We find that preparing a true health food diet often requires a considerable amount of time and trouble. It is a big commitment even if you do not go the whole hog and move to a cottage in Wales.

The nutrition establishment's cautious verdict seems to be that of course health foods can provide a good balanced diet. But any sensible varied balanced diet is just as good. We've all gained from the health food shops sprouting up among the supermarkets in the choice we all now have, if only because the extra dietary fibre from all the wholemeal is just what many of us need!

The lessons of cuisine minceur. Michel Guérard, who invented the now-famous cuisine minceur (his book is in paperback translated by Caroline Conran) took another approach. He tried to re-think all his cooking techniques in the light of what was known about healthier eating. This was no small task, since he was a chef in the great tradition of French haute cuisine and ran a very successful restaurant outside Paris. He says, in a charming introduction to his book, that he was motivated when his girl-friend suggested that he might lose a few kilos. He says, 'So I began my long trudge through acres of grated carrot and other equally agreeable delicacies, destined to push me eventually to the very edge of despair. The ritual plain grilled steak and boiled haricot verts left me gasping.'

But out of the anguish Guérard evolved his cuisine minceur. On the face of it, Guérard's ideas, now being literally fed to the rich and overweight gourmets who can afford to stay at his place in Evian les Bains, have little relevance to anyone struggling to set up house and housekeep for the first time. But if he can manage to transform the most elegant traditional French cooking, and make food that is light, delicious and a work of art, surely we can follow his example and transform our own much simpler cooking and eating habits to be much healthier?

To follow the cuisine minceur recipes requires as much commitment and dedication as following recipes for classic French dishes as described step-by-step by Julia Child. But some of his methods are very copyable. For instance, grilling rather than frying meat and fish. Cooking things 'en papillote' (in foil envelopes) instead of roasting in fat. Steaming rather than boiling vegetables, and doing it for as short a time as possible. Using marinades to tenderise and flavour meat (does wonders to a broiler chicken). His new ways of making sauces delicately but without cream. The importance he places on the quality and freshness of all the ingredients he uses. The imaginative way he serves food (a far cry from the sort of imagination which decorates with glacé cherries dyed green). All these ideas could be incorporated into home-cooking without any problem.

Guérard is not alone in sensing that we need a different, lighter kind of cooking. Other chefs in France, Bocuse and the Troisgros brothers, are doing the same thing in their own ways.

Their restaurants are very successful too. No-one has yet produced a Ms Beeton 1982 which incorporates all these ideas for you. But you'll find that they will be trickling down through cookery writers and recipe books. In twenty years' time we will all be taking them for granted.

Simplicity is now the key to entertaining
'Dinner-giving is one of the favourite methods of showing hospitality adopted by society; but rash indeed would be the host and hostess who attempted to entertain in this manner without a knowledge of dinner-party etiquette.' (*From* THE WOMAN'S BOOK, *Ed. Florence B. Jack, 1911*).

Times have changed. But you do not have to go back as far as 1911 to sense it. As recently as the early 1970s people slaved away to produce little masterpieces for their friends from Elizabeth David recipes. Iris Murdoch captures the spirit of this kind of entertaining beautifully in this description of how one of the characters, Simon, prepared a dinner in *A Fairly Honourable Defeat* (published 1970).

'Simon had after all decided against the salmon trout. They were to start with whitebait and retsina. After that a cassoulet with rice and Nuits de Young. Then a lemon sorbet. Then a salad of chicory and cos lettuce with a light dressing. Then white Stilton cheese and special wholemeal biscuits from the shop in Baker Street, with a very faintly sweetish hock.

'It was of course rather hot weather for a cassoulet but Simon especially enjoyed making this dish.'

After the oil crisis (1973) there was a reaction in favour of the home-grown, home-ground, home-made wholesome entertaining. Everyone sat round the pine table in the kitchen, as delicious stews (full of veg grown in the garden) simmered on top of the Aga (unfortunately still oil-burning) while the wholemeal home-baked goodies cooked in its oven. However the simple country life of the 1970s is almost the most time-consuming and committing of all — you have to live the life.

But who can live the simple country life (except in the country) and bustle about all day doing a job? (Even Simon, above, had had to take the afternoon off from the museum where he worked.)

Most of us have to simplify our efforts even for entertaining, if only to make time to entertain at all. And then there is the problem of expense. Who wants to feel, after seeing their friends, that they can't afford to see them, or anyone else for that matter, again for six months? Here are some ideas for entertaining without spending time and money out of all proportion to your resources.

1. Most important is to tell your guests roughly what to expect. Then their expectations are adjusted to what you are offering, whether it is the informal Sunday lunch, the cheese and wine, the barbecue and salad, the take-away Chinese buffet. In other words if they don't come expecting a Simon-style dinner, they won't be disappointed with pizza.

2. Limit your efforts. If you must cook, cook one thing well, but not anything that has to be timed to the second. This is why casseroles and quiches are so useful. (And remember almost anything can be casseroled — even vegetables.) Have with it salads. (Remembering also that almost anything can be turned into a salad.)

3. In France, they often buy dessert from the patisserie — delicious disgustingly creamy cakes or beautifully arranged fruit tarts. If there is such a patisserie near you a visit can take the strain off when you don't have time to make anything yourself.

4. The alternative is to decide to have fresh fruit in season instead.

5. At one of the best parties SK has been to recently, the food was all brought in from an Indian restaurant — who also provided the containers to keep it warm.

6. When you cater for more than eight people remember that they never eat as much as they would if they were only four. If the hostess above for example had thirty guests she could have safely reckoned that she only need order twenty-four 'meals' from the restaurant. This is especially true if it is a buffet.

7. If you provide soft drinks and mineral waters and plenty of ice, less of your expensive alcohol will be consumed because after a bit many people prefer the soft drinks.

8. As you won't be entertaining all the same people each time, you can afford to perfect a few good dishes, your party pieces, and produce them time and again until you are tired of them.

9. Look carefully at your house/flat and work out what sort of entertaining will work best in it. If you like having people to dinner and your table seats eight, stick to giving dinner parties for eight for a while. Then you can get yourself the right amount of crockery for eight, cutlery, glasses and so on. You can invest in pans and serving dishes which cook and hold enough food for eight. You'll never have to waste time wondering how to improvise another two coffee cups or where you can get hold of a pan big enough.

If, on the other hand you have a big room which could hold twenty or thirty people in comfort, you might prefer to have less frequent parties for more people. In which case you'll need rather more glasses as a matter of course. And, if you are giving them something to eat, thirty plates, knives, forks, etc., and even larger pans to cook in and dishes to serve from.

In other words, decide how you can best entertain in your home and equip yourself to do so.

10. Outdoor entertaining in this country is tricky. The number of barbecues cooked under umbrellas is probably greater than the number cooked on fine evenings. If you like barbecues, etc., it makes sense to provide yourself with some sort of fall-back arrangement under-cover.

11. One school of thought recommends having the guests work. They can do this marginally by spreading their own patés and cheeses, or dipping their crudities into your dips or fondues. Or they can actually contribute. SK finds much of the angst and hassle disappear completely if she is only responsible for one course, other people providing the other courses and some of the drink.

12. Remember that, although the point of entertaining is to make your friends happy, there is no point at all unless you are happy too! You will automatically be happier and more relaxed if you don't have to worry about the stage management because you have simplified it all for yourself.

Useful Addresses

Advisory bodies
Building Centre, 26 Store St., London, WC1.
Design Centre, 28 The Haymarket, London, W1.
Electrical Association For Women, 25 Foubert's Place, London, W1.
Incorporated Association of Architects and Surveyors, Jubilee House, Billing Brook Rd., Western Fevell, Northampton.
Royal Institute of British Architects, Clients Advisory Service, 66 Portland Place, London, W1.
Royal Institution of Chartered Surveyors, 12 Great George St., London, SW1
Solid Fuel Advisory Service, Head Office: Hobart House, Grosvenor Place, London, SW1.

Bathrooms
Barking Grohe (Biflo Taps), River Road, Barking, Essex. 1G11 0HD.
Bonsack, 14 Mount St., London, W1.
Doulton Sanitaryware Ltd., Whieldon Road, Stoke-on-Trent, ST4 4HW.
Mira (Showers), Walker Croswell & Co. Ltd., Cheltenham, Glos. CL52 5EP
Renubath Services, (London), 596 Chiswick High Rd., London, W4.
Twyfords Bathrooms, Twyfords Ltd. P.O. Box 23, Stoke-on-Trent, ST4 7AL

Electrical
Anglepoise Lighting Ltd., 51 Enfield Industrial Estate, Redditch, Worcs.
Philips Electrical, City House, 420/430 London Road, Croydon, CR9 3QR.
Trimline, Marlin Lighting, Merchant Adventurers, Hanworth Trading Estate, Rampton Road, West Feltham, Middlesex, TW13 6DR
Westinghouse Domestic Appliances, 1 Regent St., London, SW1.

Financial and Legal
British Insurance Broker's Association, Fountain's House, Fenchurch St., London, EC3.
Finance Houses Association, 18 Upper Grosvenor St., London, W1.
Incorporated Society of Valuers and Auctioneers, 3 Cadogan Gate, London, SW1.
Insurance Broker's Registration Council, 15 St. Helens Place, London, EC3.
The Law Society, 113 Chancery Lane, London, WC2.
The Law Society of Scotland, 26 Drumsheugh Gardens, Edinburgh, EH3 7YR.
National Association of Estate Agents, Walton House, 11/15 The Parade, Royal Leamington Spa, Warwick.
Rating and Valuing Association, 115 Ebury St., London, SW1.

Furniture and Furnishings.
Crown Ltd., (Anaglypta Wallcovering) Crown House, Darwen, Lancs.
Beardmore, J.D. & Co. Ltd., Ironmongers and Locksmiths, 3 Percy St., London, W1.
British Carpet Manufacturers Association, 26 St James Square, London, SW1.
Corian Distributors, Jaytee House, Enfield St., Leeds 7.
Crayonne, 81 Windmill Road, Sunbury-on-Thames, Middlesex.
Formica Information Services, Coast Road, North Shields, Tyne & Wear, WE29 8RE.
Laura Ashley, Box No 1, Mail Order Dept., Laura Ashley Ltd., Carno, Powys, Wales.
Pirelli Group, Thavies Inn House, 3 Holborn Circus., London, EC1.
Plia (Folding Chair) from branches of Habitat.
Silent-Gliss Ltd., Star Lane, Margate, Kent, CT9 4EF.
Swish Products Ltd., Lichfield Road, Tamworth, Staffs.

Heating, Ventilation and Insulation
Baxi Burnall, Dept. A6, Brownedge Rd., Bamber Bridge, Preston, Lancs.
Dimplex Heating, Marketing Dept., Millbrook, Southampton. SO9 2OP.
Duraflex (Thresholds). Kingsditch Lane, Cheltenham, Glos.

SETTING UP HOME

Esse (Stoves) Smith & Wellstood Ltd., (Dept HG2), Bonnybridge, Stirlingshire. FK4 2AP.
Gas Council, 59 Bryanston St., London, W1.
Godin (Stoves), Ellis Sykes & Son Ltd., Victoria Works, Stockport, Cheshire.
Grippa Frame, Ferry Hinksey Rd., Oxford.
Hunter Stoves, Hunter & Son (Mells) Ltd., 22 Frome, Somerset.
Jetmaster Fires Ltd., Winnall Manor Road, Winnall, Winchester, Hampshire.
Rayburn from Glynwed Domestic & Heating Appliances Ltd., Age Works, P.O. Box, Ketley, Telford, Salop. TF11 BR.
Vent-Axia, 167 London Rd., Kingston-Upon-Thames.

Kitchens
AEG-Telefunken UK Ltd., Bath Rd., Slough, SL1 4AW.
Neff Kitchen Appliances, The Quadrangle, Westmount Centre, Uxbridge Road, Hayes, Middlesex.
Omni Mini-Kitchen, Southgate Auto-Electric Ltd., Autohouse, Broomfield Lane, London, N13.
Poggenpohl, UK Ltd., (N25) 226 Tolworth Rise South, Surbiton, Surrey, KT5 9NB.
Scholtes Ltd., 2 Chase Road, Park Royal, London, NW10.
Sissons, (Sinks), Coaver Mill, Coaver Bridge, Sheffield.
Thorn Domestic Appliances (Tricity), New Lane, Havant.
Woodstock Ltd., Pakeham St., Mount Pleasant, London, WC1.

Storage
Acme Acmetrack Ltd., Holland Rd., Oxted, Surrey, RH8 9BP.
Boulton & Paul, Riverside Works, Norwich, NR1 1EB.
Channel Woodcraft Ltd., Bowles Well Gardens, Folkestone, Kent, CT19 6NP.
Dexion Ltd., Storage Equipment Manufacturers, York House, Empire Way, Wembley.
Interlübke, Unit 4, Greenwich High Rd., London, SE10.

Magnet Southern Ltd., Head Office: Magnet Joinery Ltd., Keighley, West Yorks.
Remploy (Lundia) Ltd., Lundia Division, Collinges Mill, Glodwick Rd., Oldham, O14 1BB.
Rest-Rite Bedding Co. Ltd., 51 High Road, London, NW10.
Spur (brackets) Engineering Ltd., Ascot Works, 138 Kenley Rd., London, SW19.
Tebrex (aluminium brackets), 63 Borough High St., London, SE1.
Wentelbed, Dept 18, 13/14 Golden Square, London, W1R 4EP.

Stores
ASDA ...... see Yellow pages.
Carrefour ...... see Yellow pages.
Comet ...... see Yellow Pages
Habitat, Head Office: Kings Mall, King St., London, W6.
Harrods, Brompton Road, London.
Heal's, 196 Tottenham Court Rd., London, W1.
John Lewis, Oxford St., London, W1.
M.F.I. ...... see Yellow pages.

Further Reading

Artists House, *The Apartment Book*, Mitchell Beazley.
Artists House, *Colour*, Mitchell Beazley.
Blake, Jill, *Colour and Pattern in the Home*, Design Centre Publications.
Brookes, John, *Room Outside*, Thames & Hudson.
Brookes, John, *The Small Garden*, Thames & Hudson.
Building Societies and House Purchase, Building Societies' Association.
Conran, Shirley, *Superwoman*, Penguin.
Conran, Shirley, *Superwoman in Action*, Penguin.
Conran, Terence, *The House Book*, Mitchell Beazley.
Conran, Terence, *The Kitchen Book*, Mitchell Beazley.

Consumer Association Publications:
The Which? Book of Do-It-Yourself.
The Which? Book of Money.
The Legal Side of Buying a House and Raising Money to Buy Your Home.
D.H.S.S. and H.M.S.O., *Eating for Health.*
Delbridge, Rosemary, and McAnnally, Mary, *Buy Right*, Pan.
Fingleton, Eamonn, and Tickell, Tom, *Penguin Money Book*, Penguin.
Guerard, Michel (Auth.), Conran, C. (Trans.), *Cuisine Minceur*, Macmillan.
Hopewell and Snow, *Planning your Bathroom*, Design Centre Publications.
Hunter, Lorraine, *The New Calorie Counter*, Granada.

Innes, Jocasta, *Paint Magic*, Francis Lincoln Publishers.
Innes, Jocasta, *Pauper's Home-Making Book*, Penguin.
Kron, Joan and Slesin, Suzanne, *The Industrial High Tech*, Allen Lane.
Manser and Manser, *Planning Your Kitchen*, Design Centre Publications.
Phillips, Derek, *Planning Your Lighting*, Design Centre Publications.
Radford, Penny, *Rooms for Living*, Design Centre Publications.
Reader's Digest Do-It-Yourself Manual.
Reader's Digest Repair Manual.
Reader's Digest Success with House Plants.
Wilson, Harriet, *Money Matters*, Pan.

Index

Aga cookers 10, 98, 103
amenities (neighbourhood) 29
Apartment Book 59
Art Nouveau 56
Ashley, Laura 54, 57, 59, 62, 127
auctions 139-40
    house 37

banks 13, 19-23, 141
basins *see* sinks
bathrooms 9, 55-6, 111-17, 120, 127
    en suite 110
baths 114
bedclothes 106-7
bedrooms 105-10
beds 79-81, 105-6
bidet 116
blinds 55, 64, 78, 112, 133
Boulton & Paul 64, 85, 101
Bowmans 54
British Insurance Brokers
    Association 22
British Standards 61
Brookes, J. 122-3
Building Centres 48
building societies 13, 14, 18, 19, 22-3, 141-2
Building Societies and House Purchase 18
Building Societies Association 18, 23
    Support Scheme 20
building-in 77, 108 *see also* cupboards, shelves, units
building-on 10
buying a house 13-26
Buying Your Own Home 32

carpets 54, 58, 63, 92, 96, 109, 130 *see also* floors
cash-and-carry stores 146-7
ceilings 55-6, 125-6
Cement and Concrete Association 122
chairs 82-3, 91-2 *see also* sofas, divans
Channel Woodcraft 64
chimneys 39
    kits 90
'circulation' 67, 70
Citizens Advice Bureau 26, 145
coal *see* solid fuel

Coles Bros. 57, 59, 62-3
Colour 59
colour, use of 54-5, 57-62, 104, 112
    schemes 68, 78
completion day 37
Conran Designs 59
conservatories 10
Consumer's Association 20, 137
consumer's rights 143-5
contract to buy 35-7
conveyancing 25, 35-6
cookers 86-7, 98
cottages 57-8, 60, 105
credit 140-3
credit cards 141
cuisine minceur 153-4
cupboards 10, 54-6, 65, 84-5, 114 *see also* shelving, storage
    airing 133-4
curtains 46, 55-6, 64, 68, 84, 112, 131-3
cushions, floor 91-2

Dalton's Weekly 32
damp 39-41, 46, 48
damp-proof course 39-41
Design Centre 59, 136-7
    Index 115, 136
Designer's Guild 54, 59
diets 150-1
dining rooms 69 *see also* kitchens, living rooms
discount stores 138
divans 79, 91-2
dividers, room 77
D-I-Y 30, 84-5, 108, 114, 125-35
doors 40-1, 46, 56, 65, 103, 124
    moving location of 70
    sliding 89
double glazing 9, 44, 46, 64, 133 *see also* insulation (windows)
drains 41-2, 117

Eating for Health 150
Edwardian houses 55-6, 94, 105, 108
electricity 42-3, 47-8, 51
energy, ambient 48
entertaining 154-6
estate agents 10, 12, 30-1

Exchange and Mart 32

fabric (of a building) 39
fences 124
finance houses 20
fireplaces 9, 49, 71, 90, 92
floors 41, 47, 54-7, 63, 95-6, 102, 109-12, 129-31 *see also* carpets
focal points (of rooms) 92
foundations 40
freezer centres 147
fridges 98
friendly societies 22
friezes 63-4, 127
fuels 9, 47 *see also* solid fuels, electricity, gas
furniture 54-5, 58, 61, 108 *see also* beds, chairs, tables
    outdoor 122-3

gallery 81-2
garage 10, 72, 124
Garden Cities 53
gardens 9, 118-24
gas 43-4, 47, 50 *see also* heating
    bottled 47
guarantees 143-4
Guérard, M. 153-4
Guild, T. 132

Habitat 54, 59, 62, 91, 104
hanging baskets 120-1
Heals 54, 59, 102
health foods 152-3
heaters 43 *see also* night storage heaters
heating 9, 44, 47, 49-51, 90, 112-13
High Tech 55, 81, 84
hire purchase 142
Homefinder 32
Homeloan Scheme 22-3
hot water cylinder insulation 133
House and Garden 59, 118
house-hunting 27-38
    where to look 30-2
house types *see* semis, modern, Victorian, Edwardian, cottages, terraces
House-buyer 32

housekeeping 136-56
house plans 67-8, 74, 97-8
housing estates 32
hydroculture 120

Incorporated Society of Valuers and Auctioneers 24, 31
Innes, J. 126, 130
Institute of Electrical Engineers 43
insulation 9, 40-1, 44-5, 49, 64, 103, 133-4
   cold water tank 45
   doors 46, 103, 133
   floors 47
   roof 45, 72, 133
   walls 46
   windows 46, 103, 133 see also double glazing
insurance brokers 21-2
Insurance Brokers Registration Council 22
insurance companies 20
insurance company loans 142-3
insurance policy loans 142
investment 8, 13
   things which don't repay 9-10
   things which repay 8-9
ironmongery 64-5, 124

jacuzzis 10, 111

kitchen equipment 83-4, 87
kitchens 9, 54-6, 69, 71, 78, 83, 86-7, 97-104, 120, 127
   micro 86-7

Land Registry 25
larders 71
Law Society 26
Liberty 59, 64
lighting 60, 62, 65-6, 78, 95, 102-3, 108-9, 112, 124
limescale 114
living rooms 89-96
local authorities 32, 41
   grants 39
   mortgages 20
   planning permission 69, 71, 117
   plans 29

Magnet 64, 85, 101
markets 148
meters 43-4
miniaturise 86-7
mirrors 65, 68, 78, 109
modern houses 54-5, 105, 124
Money Which? 14
Morris, William 56, 61
mortgage broker 20-1
mortgages 13-22, 35, 77
   endowment 16-17
   factors affecting 18-19
   option repayment 16-17
   repayment 16-17
moving (what must be left) 11

National Association of Estate Agents 31
National Girobank 22
National House Builders Council (NHBC) 25
National Savings Bank 22, 24
neighbourhoods 9-10
New Calorie Counter 150
new town development corporations 20-1
night storage heaters 49, 51
nutrition 148-52

offer, how to make an 34-5
oil 48, 50-1 see also fuels
Oliver, J. 62
one-room living 73-88
Osborne & Little 59
outbuildings 124
outgoings test 14
'own-brand' appliances 138
Oxfam shops 64

Paint Magic 126, 130
painting 63-4, 112, 125-6, 130
paraffin stoves 48
patios 9, 122
patterns 62 see also Laura Ashley, William Morris
paving 122
Philips Colour 80 62, 102, 112, 120
pianos 94
pied-a-terres 73 see also one-room living
plants 61, 118-24
plumbing 111, 115, 117 see also drains, sinks, baths, WC
Poggenpohl 97, 102
P-Y-O fruit and veg 147-8

Rating and Valuing Association 31
Reader's Digest publications 8, 118, 122, 126-8, 134-5
refrigerators see fridges
roof space 71-2
roofs 39, 45-6 see also insulation (roof)
Room Outside 122-3
rot 45-6 see also damp
Royal Institute of Chartered Surveyors (RICS) 24, 31
rugs see carpets

Sanderson 59, 127
sanding see floors
saving (where to) 22-4
Scotland, house buying in 38
searches 36
seating 90-2 see also chairs, sofas, divans
secondhand goods 139
semis 53-4, 105, 124
shelving 10, 54-5, 58, 85-6, 92-5, 134-5
   book 94
shopping 146-8

shops 28 see also markets, supermarkets, P-Y-O, freezer centres, cash-and-carry
showers 42, 116, 155
sinks 99, 114-5
The Small Garden 123
sofas 80-1, 90-2
Soft Furnishings 132
solar panels 9, 48-9
solicitors 25-6, 35-7
solid fuel 48, 50-1, 90
Solid Fuel Advisory Service 48, 144
stairs, changing 69-70
stamp duty 25
'starter homes' 30-1
storage 84, 100-1, 103, 107-8, 113 see also cupboards, shelving, units
   open 85-6
structural changes 69-70, 89
studio flats 73 see also one-room living
style 52-66
supermarkets 147
survey 24-5, 35, 39, 40
   your own 33-4

tables 82, 92-4
tax 15-17
televisions 86, 92, 110
tender, buying by 37-8
terrace houses 57-8, 124
thermostatic controls 50
tiling 135
trade associations 144
transport 29-30
Trustee Savings Bank 22

Ulster Savings Bank 22
units 10, 91, 101
utility room 72

valuation fee 23-4
ventilation 78, 102, 113
Victorian houses 55-6, 105

WC 111, 113, 116
wallpapering 63, 112, 126-8
walls 39-40, 46, 63-4, 125-6 see also insulation
Warners 57, 59
waste disposer 86
water supplies 42, 98-9 see also drains, plumbing
Which? magazines 14, 98, 115, 137
window boxes 120-1, 124
windows 40-1, 46, 64, 103
   enlarging 70-1
without-profits scheme 17
with-profits scheme (endowment mortgage) 17
woodwork 57, 60, 124, 128-9
worktops 99-100

Yudkin, J. 150